wisdom FOR life

THE HEALING POWER OF

FORGIVENESS

*Peaceful Hearts and Minds,
Healed Relationships, and
Freedom from Bitter Resentment
through the Restoring Power
of Forgiveness.*

GEORGE FOSTER

Copyright © 2008 by George Foster

ISBN 978-1-934770-26-9

American edition published by Summerside Press,
11024 Quebec Circle, Bloomington, MN 55438, USA.
Part of the Wisdom for Life series.

First published in 1993 in Portuguese as *Perdão Já!* by Editora Betânia S/C
Caixa Postal 5010 – 31611-970 Venda Nova, MG, Brazil.

Subsequent editions in Portuguese have the title *O Poder Restaurador do Perdão.*
Translated by Myrian Tlitha Lins.

*Summerside Press™ is an inspirational publisher offering fresh, irresistible books
to uplift the heart and delight the mind.*

Printed in China.

TABLE OF CONTENTS

" 'YOU WILL KNOW THE TRUTH, AND THE TRUTH WILL SET YOU FREE.' "

JOHN 8:32

INTRODUCTION

What I am seeking to offer you in this book is freedom from bitterness, resentment, and recurring feelings of worthlessness that come as an aftermath of the disappointment and pain you have suffered.

I want you to understand that forgiveness is not just a once-and-for-all emotion. It is a choice taken with God's help and a process of healing that enables you to be free—not from the memory but from the pain of your suffering.

You should not have to go on with the complicated feelings of guilt and self-accusation that result from having made a decision to forgive but experiencing ongoing feelings of resentment.

" 'IF YOU DO NOT FORGIVE MEN THEIR SINS, YOUR FATHER WILL NOT FORGIVE YOUR SINS.' "

MATTHEW 6:15

FORGIVE OR...

A SEVENTEEN-YEAR-OLD GIRL once appeared on the Oprah Winfrey Show, facing before TV cameras the violent man who, four years earlier, had beaten her beyond recognition and left her to die. After seventeen operations for facial reconstruction, her words to the vicious attacker were, "I don't hate you. I hate what you did to me, and I have had to forgive you so I could go on with my life."

Before she ever got to the television studio, she had made the right decision—the intelligent, redemptive decision—that would enable her to not only face her attacker, but also to face life with peace of heart and emotional freedom from the suffering she had known.

That is not to say that her decision was an easy one; it was a difficult choice to make, and it would be a difficult one to maintain. It would require an ongoing healing process and a commitment to reaffirm her decision every time her suffering came to mind. Still, in light of the fact that her whole life was before her, her future was opened in a way she could never know had she not decided to forgive.

WE ALL GET HURT

Few of us will ever face what this young woman has, but we have our own issues! We have our hurts. We have our complaints. In a world filled with conflict and pain, it is almost certain that you and I have been—or will be—deceived, injured, cheated, betrayed, slighted, rejected, or in some other way hurt. Then what?

Unless we forgive the persons who hurt us, we could find ourselves emotionally and spiritually crippled for the rest of our lives. An act of forgiveness can be the decisive step in solving both emotional and physical problems.

Forgiveness is the effective solution for relationship issues both in our personal lives and in society. The ability to forgive, keep on forgiving, *and know we have forgiven* is a constant challenge. More than that, it is an attainable source of strength and peace!

Forgiveness may be the most difficult gift we can offer to anyone, and, ironically, it must be offered to those who least deserve it—aggressors, offenders, and injurers, whether intentional or not. And here's the twist: We do it for our own good!

My interest in the subject of forgiveness is both personal and pastoral—personal because I, too, have been betrayed, and pastoral because I have been called upon to help people with their issues of bitterness and pain. The willingness to forgive brings God's help into situations that seem overwhelming and hopeless, and they can become the most precious lessons we will ever learn.

AN OVERNIGHT RIDE WITH A BETRAYER

My most memorable experience with forgiveness took place one cold night as I rode an overnight sleeper bus from São Paulo, Brazil, where I had been on business, to that nation's third largest city, Belo Horizonte, where I lived. It was my second straight night on the bus, and though I should have been able to sleep, I could not.

Instead, I agonized over a betrayal I had suffered at the hands of a person whom I called a friend. I struggled with angry, bitter thoughts toward him. Oh, I had already decided to forgive him, but my decision was made too hastily—without much thought for what he had done and without reflection on how deeply I felt the pain. I had tried to minimize the situation and forgive out of a sense of Christian duty based on the following logic: He betrayed me. I am a Christian. Christians forgive; therefore I forgive him.

Now it came back to haunt me. I will not go into details about his offense because I have learned that in order to maintain an attitude of ongoing forgiveness, I must not tell people what he did. I never have, and I never will.

That night as I lay in the reclining seat—unable to sleep, unable to get up, and unable to think of anything but the disloyalty I had suffered—I realized that the man who had hurt me was traveling with me. In fact, for several weeks he rarely left my thoughts or emotions. I often felt angry and resentful. If he had suddenly appeared on the bus in person, something might have happened that a missionary should not be a part of!

Then I heard the silent-but-persistent voice of Satan, "the accuser," saying, "If you had truly forgiven him, you wouldn't feel the way you do now!"

So not only did I feel hurt and angry, I felt sinful and condemned for not forgiving. (Have you been there before?)

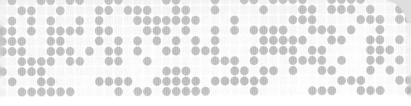

Seeking to be rational, I said to myself, "Well, if I haven't forgiven him before, I forgive him now!"

That was helpful for a time, but it didn't provide answers for my confusion regarding *decisions* to forgive and concurrent *feelings* of unforgiveness. I guess I thought that the decision to forgive would somehow work in me the miracle of instant and permanent freedom from the pain I felt—but believe me, it didn't.

I discovered that every time I allowed myself to think about what this person had done, I relived the emotions and anger returned to my heart. So I had to be careful what I thought, what I said, and what I did.

THE TRUTH WE NEED

Many Bible texts teach us to control our thoughts, words, and actions. I have chosen the following verses from Ephesians 4:29–32 to guide me through times like the one I was having:

> *"Do not let any unwholesome talk come out of your mouths,*
> *but only what is helpful for building others up according to their*
> *needs, that it may benefit those who listen. And do not grieve the*

Holy Spirit of God, with whom you were sealed for the day of redemption. Get rid of all bitterness, rage and anger, brawling and slander, along with every form of malice. Be kind and compassionate to one another, forgiving each other, just as in Christ God forgave you."

God's Word tells us what to do, what to say, and even what to think about, but it does not specifically command us as to what we should feel. It was liberating for me to understand that feelings are essentially *involuntary reactions or responses* to actions, words, thoughts, and happenings. We should never accept condemnation based purely upon our feelings. We can only control our feelings by doing, saying, and thinking what is right.

WHY FORGIVENESS?

Unless we forgive, we experience ongoing anger, bitterness, conflict, distress, dysfunction, hatred, and hostility, along with mental and emotional instability and possible physical illness. Ironically, we may experience more pain from our ongoing attitudes than we did from the offense that originated the pain. And we may experience *much more* pain than the person we are trying to punish by refusing to forgive them.

As I consider the need for forgiveness, I like to follow what I think is a biblically sound and logically arranged sequence of realities:

1. WE LIVE IN A WORLD THAT BRINGS US TROUBLE AND CONFLICT. " 'In this world you will have trouble. But take heart! I have overcome the world' " (John 16:33). A very real and devilish kingdom of darkness conflicts with God's kingdom of light. As we respond to the Light, we are transformed. Depending upon the stage of our journey from darkness to light, we may experience confusion.

2. WE MAY BE BETRAYED OR ATTACKED OR OFFENDED OR WRONGED OR WOUNDED. Brother will betray brother, a father his children, and children their parents (see Matthew 10:21). We will never fully understand this until we're in heaven. Mistakes, accidents, and tragedies happen, sometimes with nothing or no one to blame. Sometimes we suffer while doing right and others prosper while doing wrong.

3. TO RECOVER, WE MUST FULLY FORGIVE THOSE WHO WOUND US. " 'If you forgive men...your heavenly Father will also forgive you' " (Matthew 6:14). Forgiveness is the tool for repairing our battered emotions. We may wish to be free from individuals who hurt us, but they only leave our troubled spirits in peace once we forgive them.

4. SEVERE PAIN, SERIOUS DAMAGE, AND CONSTANT ANNOYANCE ARE HARD TO FORGIVE. "How many times must I forgive?" (Matthew 18:21 NCV). We may experience more pain from ongoing, unforgiving attitudes than we did from the offense that first originated the pain.

5. FORGIVENESS MUST REACH EACH OF THE INJURED PERSONS. "Be kind and compassionate to one another, forgiving each other" (Ephesians 4:32). We must forgive those who hurt us, ask forgiveness of those we hurt, and forgive ourselves.

6. NOT JUST A FEELING, FORGIVENESS IS A DECISION, A COMMITMENT, AND A PROCESS. "How many times?... Seventy times seven!" (i.e., countless times). (See Matthew 18:22.) We must free offenders of emotional debts and work on our inner reactions until we, too, are free.

7. JESUS SET THE EXAMPLE AND THE STANDARD BY FORGIVING THOSE WHO CRUCIFIED HIM. "Father, forgive them, for they do not know what they are doing" (Luke 23:34). As we receive forgiveness in Christ, we must offer forgiveness to others as He did to us.

8. MOST IMPORTANTLY, JESUS CAN EMPOWER US

TO FORGIVE AS HE DID. "I can do all things through Christ who strengthens me" (Philippians 4:13 NKJV). God's Spirit pours His love into our hearts and enables us to love and forgive. We must ask and believe.

9. WE RECOVER PEACE, JOY, AND STABILITY AS WE OBTAIN AND MAINTAIN A FORGIVING SPIRIT.

"Forgiving each other, just as in Christ God forgave you" (Ephesians 4:32). We must lay down our arms and grievances and leave them there.

10. WE ARE CALLED TO BE GOD'S INSTRUMENTS OF FORGIVENESS, PEACE, AND RECONCILIATION.

"He has committed to us the ministry of reconciliation" (2 Corinthians 5:19). Our experiences of peace and freedom affect those around us.

RELATIONSHIPS: RICH OR RISKY?

When I was a young man and studying to be a missionary, our college leaders often brought visiting missionaries to speak about problems we might face in cross-cultural mission settings. They were especially interested in warning us about issues that could cause missionaries to give up and leave the field—a major concern to every missionary organization. We could almost predict what the speakers would say: "Your biggest problem will not be the culture, language, food, customs, climate, or adverse conditions. Your major difficulty will be related to getting along with your missionary colleagues."

Quite frankly, I didn't believe them. I wondered why the persons responsible didn't select speakers who knew more about getting along with people. Let me make it clear: *I do believe them now!* I have believed them for forty years—ever since I went to the mission field and, three weeks after my arrival, found myself in a disagreement with one of my colleagues.

We like to talk about lofty spiritual subjects such as...

—LOVING GOD WITH ALL OUR BEINGS AND LOVING OUR
  NEIGHBORS AS OURSELVES, AS DIRECTED IN LUKE 10:27;
—ACHIEVING UNITY IN THE BODY OF CHRIST TO INCREASE THE
  EFFECTIVENESS OF OUR WORK AND TO SET A CONVINCING
  EXAMPLE TO A WORLD THAT NEEDS TO BELIEVE;
—LIVING A JOYFUL EXPERIENCE OF PEACEFUL RELATIONSHIPS
  WITH FAMILY AND FRIENDS.

These are essential concepts, but let's face it: None of this is possible unless we learn to offer and receive forgiveness. There is much to learn. Even though the need for forgiveness is easily understood and the principles are well-known, the practical applications are subjective and filled with emotional distress. They often get left undone.

I am not a trained psychologist. I have spent my adult life as a pastor and am now a pastor to pastors and missionaries. I have learned that everyone needs to be forgiven and needs to forgive. Everyone needs to learn more about forgiveness and make it a permanent, restorative part of their daily lives.

Please take this message personally. God wants you to be a forgiven and forgiving person. He calls you to it, holds you to it, and will empower you to do it.

" 'FORGIVE US OUR DEBTS,
AS WE ALSO HAVE
FORGIVEN OUR DEBTORS.' "

MATTHEW 6:12

BE FORGIVEN
AND BE FORGIVING

WHEN *THE PASSION OF THE CHRIST* hit the
theaters, everyone talked about the violence. Dolly and
I wanted to see the film, but we weren't looking forward to all
the bloodshed. We decided to wait awhile before making up
our minds.

Then one night our son called from São Paulo, Brazil, where
he lives with his wife. "Dad, you have to see this film!" he said.

Curious about his enthusiasm, I asked, "Why do you
think we should we go? What effect did it have on you?"

His answer was surprising and convincing: "It made me
feel that I never want to do anything wrong again." We made
immediate plans to attend.

After the showing, Dolly and I left the theater in silence. Under the impact of the vivid scenes, neither of us felt able to speak. Nobody was speaking. Later Dolly said, "What got to me was when Jesus was undergoing such suffering and He said, 'Father, forgive them; for they know not what they do' " (see Luke 23:34).

FORGIVENESS IS THE ISSUE

Why all that suffering? The Lord Jesus Christ, God's Son, came into this world to take upon Himself the sin and suffering of all humanity and make atonement for us on the cross—so that we could be forgiven, healed, and restored to a relationship with God. That's the gospel truth! Jesus does not ask us to atone for our sins or for the sins of others, but He does ask us to offer forgiveness to those who sin against us just as He offers forgiveness to us. From His point of view, the forgiveness we receive and the forgiveness we offer to others are, of necessity, linked. He kept repeating, "We are forgiven, so we forgive" and "We forgive, so we are forgiven."

Jesus spoke in surprising ways about forgiveness. His teaching is extremely vivid and demanding. Consider the force and importance of the following verses, each extracted from a larger passage regarding forgiveness:

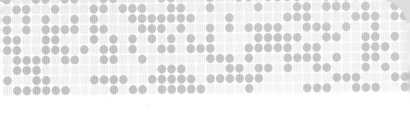

....

" 'And when you stand praying, if you hold anything against anyone, forgive him, so that your Father in heaven may forgive you your sins' " (MARK 11:25).

" 'If your brother sins, rebuke him, and if he repents, forgive him. If he sins against you seven times in a day, and seven times comes back to you and says, "I repent," forgive him' "
(LUKE 17:3–4).

....

RECEIVING FORGIVENESS

In Luke 5:17–26, Jesus was teaching in His hometown of Nazareth and, as He taught, people in the crowd were being healed of their sicknesses and diseases. Seeing this, four of the village men thought of a paralytic friend of theirs and carried him to the meeting place, where they hoped he might be healed.

Arriving at the house where Jesus was teaching, they encountered a crowd so tightly packed that they were not able to get in. Desperately they climbed to the rooftop, calculated where Jesus was standing below, pulled off the roof tiles, and lowered their friend on a mat into the presence of the Lord.

The man had probably survived by begging in a public place, and it's possible that everyone present knew about his paralysis. Only Jesus seemed to perceive and care about a deeper need. The crowd was shocked when Jesus, instead of pronouncing words of healing, said, "Friend, your sins are forgiven" (verse 20 NCV).

Certain religious leaders objected and commented quietly among themselves that Jesus was being blasphemous, because no one could forgive sins except God. Then Jesus said to the paralyzed man, "Stand up, take your mat, and go home" (verse 4 NCV). And to everyone's amazement, the man stood to his feet for the first time in his life and walked out—healed and forgiven!

What wonderful insights we find in this story. It tells us that…

1. MORE THAN PHYSICAL HEALING, OUR GREATEST NEED IS FORGIVENESS. It's possible that the man was reconciled to lying on that mat for the rest of his life but could not bear living another minute without being reconciled to God. We all have sinned. We all need forgiveness.

2. JESUS CHRIST HAS THE AUTHORITY TO FORGIVE OUR SINS. You and I can forgive people for what they do to us, but only Jesus can offer the pardon to establish or restore our right-standing before God.

3. WHEN JESUS FORGIVES US, HE LOVES TO ASSURE US THAT WE ARE FORGIVEN. In His frequent saving encounters with various individuals, He chose clear words to let them know that they were then forgiven:

....

"Friend, your sins are forgiven" (LUKE 5:20).

"Neither do I condemn you; go and sin no more" (JOHN 8:11 NKJV).

"Today you will be with me in paradise" (LUKE 23:43).

"Today salvation has come to this house" (LUKE 19:9).

"Your faith has saved you; go in peace" (LUKE 7:50).

....

He still loves to unequivocally assure us that our sins are forgiven.

4. WITH FORGIVENESS, WE MAY ALSO EXPERIENCE PHYSICAL AND EMOTIONAL HEALING. Though perhaps not the case with the paralytic man, many illnesses of the body and mind are directly related to problems of the spirit and soul. Dealing with the spiritual issues often brings breakthroughs in the physical realm.

5. NO PROBLEM IS TOO HARD FOR JESUS TO SOLVE. Jesus made it clear that He had the authority and power to declare, "You are forgiven" and "Get up and walk." Nothing is too hard for Him. Forgiveness and healing are blessings that many people need and receive today.

6. THE BEST THING WE CAN DO FOR OURSELVES AND FOR OUR FRIENDS IS TO GET TO JESUS.

Wonderful things can happen in Christ's presence when we look to Him and have faith.

There is nothing more important in this life for us to tend to than the salvation of our eternal souls. Maybe we assume that we are forgiven because we're like a lot of other nice people. Or perhaps we just hope we are forgiven. Jesus wants to give us the strong biblical assurance that we are forgiven. All of us would love to hear the words "Friend, your sins are forgiven" directly from the lips of Jesus. What greater assurance could there be? It's the assurance we can have.

OFFERING FORGIVENESS TO OTHERS

Jesus taught His disciples that it is not enough to be forgiven; they must also forgive:

"If you forgive men when they sin against you, your heavenly Father will also forgive you. But if you do not forgive men their sins, your Father will not forgive your sins" (MATTHEW 6:12–15).

An unforgiving heart is incapable of truly receiving forgiveness. The connection between forgiveness received and forgiveness offered to others is spelled out dramatically in a dialogue that Jesus had with Peter in Matthew 18:21–35. This impulsive disciple may have been tired of the offenses a colleague committed and asked, " 'Lord, how many times shall I forgive my brother when he sins against me? Up to seven times?' "

Jesus answered, " 'I tell you, not seven times, but seventy-seven times.' " This number, sometimes cited as "seventy times seven," apparently is meant "as many times as is necessary."

Then Jesus went on to illustrate his point with a story:

. . . .

" *The kingdom of heaven is like a king who wanted to settle accounts with his servants. As he began the settlement, a man who owed him ten thousand talents was brought to him. Since he was not able to pay, the master ordered that he and his wife and his children and all that he had be sold to repay the debt.*

The servant fell on his knees before him. "Be patient with me," he begged, "and I will pay back everything."

The servant's master took pity on him, canceled the debt and let him go.

But when that servant went out, he found one of his fellow servants who owed him a hundred denarii. He grabbed him and began to choke him. "Pay back what you owe me!" he demanded.

His fellow servant fell to his knees and begged him, "Be patient with me, and I will pay you back."

But he refused. Instead, he went off and had the man thrown into prison until he could pay the debt.

When the other servants saw what had happened, they were greatly distressed and went and told their master everything that had happened.

Then the master called the servant in. "You wicked servant," he said, "I canceled all that debt of yours because you begged me to. Shouldn't you have had mercy on your fellow servant just as I had on you?"

In anger his master turned him over to the jailers to be tortured, until he should pay back all he owed.

This is how my heavenly Father will treat each of you unless you forgive your brother from your heart.' "

....

Isn't it incredible that a man could be forgiven such a large debt and then refuse to forgive such a small one!

Do you suppose that he...

—DIDN'T UNDERSTAND THAT HE WAS FULLY AND FOREVER FORGIVEN?

—THOUGHT HE WOULD HAVE TO PAY AT A LATER DATE?
(HE OFFERED.)

—THOUGHT HE COULD PAY BY HIS OWN SCHEMES?

—THOUGHT HE SHOULD MAKE A TOKEN EFFORT TO PAY?

—WAS TOO PROUD TO ADMIT HOW POOR AND HELPLESS
HE WAS?

—HAD OTHER DEBTS HE HAD NEVER REVEALED?

—DISTRUSTED THE CHARACTER OF THE KING?

DEBT-FREE LIVING

For whatever reason, he was a deeply indebted man who was released from all his financial obligations. He had a fresh start, but he wasn't prepared for it. The same greed that had put him into debt now motivated him to demand an insignificant amount from a colleague. Not only did his attitude injure the poor colleague, but it brought about his own imprisonment and torture.

What kind of torture do we experience when we don't forgive? Author and pastor David Seamands explains that when we fail to forgive, we often suffer from hidden tormentors like sickness, guilt, mental distress, insomnia, eating disorders, chemical dependence, self-hatred, self-destructive behavior, and personal conflicts.[1]

LET'S TALK ABOUT DEBT

In "The Lord's Prayer" we are taught to pray, "Forgive us our sins [debts], for we also forgive everyone who sins against us [debtors]" (Luke 11:4). Paul instructs us:

....

"Give everyone what you owe him: If you owe taxes, pay taxes; if revenue, then revenue; if respect, then respect; if honor, then honor. Let no debt remain outstanding, except the continuing debt to love one another, for he who loves his fellowman has fulfilled the law" (ROMANS 13:7–8).

....

To the degree that we increase awareness of and appreciation for the forgiveness we receive, we increase in ability to forgive as we have been forgiven. Mercy begets mercy. Like no one else in this world, those who have experienced the mercy and forgiveness of God are qualified and become responsible to offer that mercy to others. If this story tells us anything, it says that for our own good and for our personal freedom, we must forgive those who have debts they owe us. I don't think that means we should cancel all business debts that people owe (although that may sometimes be appropriate) but we should cancel all records and resentment of offenses committed against us.

Yes, the person may have a debt to pay, but we have a debt,

as well. As the apostle so clearly states, if we have experienced the love of God, we have a debt of love to pay to everyone:

....

"Since God so loved us, we also ought to love one another"
(1 JOHN 4:11).

"We love because He first loved us" (1 JOHN 4:19)

"Whoever loves God must also love his brother" (1 JOHN 4:21).

....

It's not a trade-off. We don't love to pay for love. We don't forgive to pay for forgiveness. We love and forgive in response to the love and forgiveness we have received. The forgiveness we offer is an indicator that we truly have been healthily forgiven. If we find ourselves unwilling to forgive, perhaps we need to make sure that we have fully accepted the forgiveness that Christ offers to us. This is not something we can earn or deserve; it is something that we must humbly and gratefully receive.

However we look at it, the challenge to forgive people who hurt us is one that—with God's help—we can rise to and achieve. The more we experience the love and forgiveness of God, the better equipped we will be to love and forgive others.

"IF WE CONFESS
OUR SINS,
HE...WILL FORGIVE."

1 JOHN 1:9

FORGIVENESS
FOR THE FORGIVEN

WHEN I LIVED IN BRAZIL and wrote magazine articles
in Portuguese, a troubled young follower of Jesus wrote to me.
Here's the translation of his letter:

....

*"I have a problem. Four months ago my girlfriend and I were
converted to Christ. Before our conversion, we had sex together
regularly. Since then we have tried to stop, but several times we
have fallen. Each time I feel guilty and angry at myself, but it
happens again and again.*

*I sought counsel with our pastor, and he told me to confess
my sin before the whole church. It was very hard, but I did
what he said and my happiness returned. Sadly, though,*

within a week, we sinned again. At that point I thought there was no hope for me and that I might as well go back to the life I had lived before. But I know that is exactly what Satan wants. One night I told my girlfriend how I felt—that if the Lord should come for me, I wouldn't be ready.

What I want you to answer is this: Has God forgiven us? Sometimes I think God doesn't love us. I'm afraid He will punish me. I often feel like a worthless animal.

Please be frank with me. After confessing Christ and falling into sin again, is there forgiveness for us? Is our name written in the Book of Life? I beg an answer of you."

....

I remember thinking, *There is something about the honesty of this young man that I like!* No beating around the bush. No excuses. No blaming the other person—or anyone else! I took time to write him the answer I thought he deserved and certainly needed. I hope it helped him.

BUT I HAD SOME QUESTIONS OF MY OWN

WHY SHOULD THEY HAVE TO CONFESS THEIR SIN BEFORE THE WHOLE CHURCH? Public confession is appropriate in some situations. Scripture does say: "Confess

your sins to each other and pray for each other so that you may be healed" (James 5:16). I know that public confession may be necessary when the offender is a church leader and public knowledge of the offense compromises the testimony of the church. But since this young couple's sins were committed in private, since they were new Christians, and since they were serious and sincere enough to seek help from their pastor, I don't know why the pastor couldn't have worked with them in a more discreet manner. Confessing before the entire church certainly didn't do any lasting good. I wish the pastor had been guided by the rule of thumb I like to follow: Make the confession as public as the sin was.

COULDN'T THEY JUST GET MARRIED? Perhaps that was where their relationship was going. Scripture does say: "If they cannot control themselves, they should marry, for it is better to marry than to burn with passion" (1 Corinthians 7:9). But let's say they do marry: Will marriage resolve their feelings of guilt about the past? Will marriage free them from sin? And is the avoidance of sin the best reason to get married? What if they are not right for each other? Their marriage will undoubtedly be affected by their sin—unless they find a way to repent, become assured of God's forgiveness, and are able to forgive themselves and each other.

WHY DON'T THEY STOP SEEING EACH OTHER UNTIL THEY CAN FIND STRENGTH TO RESIST THEIR SEXUAL URGES? This would make sense if time spent away from each other really did strengthen their resolve or weaken their desire, but it might have the opposite effect— to strengthen their desire and weaken their resolve.

COULD THEY BECOME ACCOUNTABLE TO A MATURE, TRUSTWORTHY CHRISTIAN COUPLE THAT WOULD PROVIDE ENCOURAGEMENT AND ACCOUNTABILITY AND GUIDE THEM THROUGH THEIR STRUGGLES? That would certainly be helpful, and I recommended it. Getting some tough love from mentors is a tremendous blessing.

THE QUESTIONS BEHIND THE QUESTIONS

But I'm not trying to solve their problem here. I want to focus on the questions that may be behind the ones the young man asked and that many Christians also ask:

1. **AM I FORGIVEN IF I CAN'T STOP SINNING?**

2. **AM I FORGIVEN IF I DON'T FEEL FORGIVEN?**

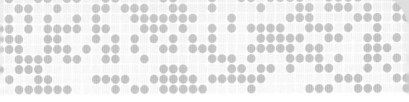

3. IS GOD ANGRY AT ME?

4. DOES HE STILL LOVE AND ACCEPT ME?

5. HAVE I COMMITTED THE UNPARDONABLE SIN?

IN THE HEAD
BUT NOT IN THE HEART

In my opinion the short answers are:

1. WHO SAYS YOU CAN'T STOP SINNING? GOD CAN PROVIDE THE GRACE TO HELP YOU CHANGE.

2. BEING FORGIVEN DOESN'T DEPEND ON FEELING FORGIVEN.

3. NO, I BELIEVE THAT GOD FEELS COMPASSION AND EXTENDS MERCY TO YOU.

4. GOD'S MERCY EXISTS TO BRING YOU TO REPENTANCE AND VICTORY.

5. YOU HAVEN'T COMMITTED "THE UNPARDONABLE SIN"!

My letter of response included all of these statements, and perhaps that should suffice. I have observed, however, that many Christians who have no trouble accepting answers like these in theory are unable to apply them to themselves and believe them in practice. Countless believers are plagued by doubts, guilt, and shame for sins they have committed—even though they have prayed for forgiveness once, twice, a thousand times. They *hope* they are forgiven. They *say* they are forgiven. But in their hearts they are not sure.

A few years ago, I was part of a group of people who attempted to counsel a young woman from another country who had served as a missionary in India. She left the field because she thought she had committed the "unpardonable sin"—though she would never tell us what it was. A dedicated group of Christians prayed for her and supported her. She seemed to cling to our prayers but couldn't embrace our counsel in her heart. Tragically, she lost hope and, to our horror, took her own life.

One more experience: I was in Europe, speaking to a group of young missionaries. An attractive young woman in the group had taken a vacation, met a former boyfriend, and plunged into two weeks of sexual encounters—not casually, but obsessively. When her vacation was over, since she had a commitment to fulfill with the mission, she returned to her work. She was willing to do her "Christian duty" but feared that she would never again have true fellowship with God. When God's Word convinced her that there is forgiveness and restoration for those who practice even shameful behavior, she could truly repent of the error and believe that her fellowship with God was restored.

Why did she feel her sin so deeply? Why so much guilt and shame? Let me say what many people don't want to hear: She felt guilt and shame because she *needed* to feel guilty, and she *needed* to be ashamed of what she had done. She was created to feel that way after committing the sins she did. It was the depth of her conviction, sorrow, guilt, and shame that made it possible for her to feel the same depth of repentance, forgiveness, and cleansing once she responded to God's grace as she did! She was humbled, broken, and thoroughly repentant. I'm convinced that she had a life-changing experience of forgiveness and cleansing that brought her the strength to overcome new temptations that would come her way. She was like the woman to whom Jesus said, "Go, and sin no more" (John 8:11).

Now let me ask...

WERE THESE YOUNG PEOPLE REALLY CONVERTED TO CHRIST?

Some Christians can't believe that people who commit these kinds of sin have truly been converted to Christ. Others think that if they ever were converted, they have abandoned or lost their faith—especially the girl who ended her own life. Only God truly knows.

Each of them had moral breakdowns and deep psychological and spiritual needs, but they were seeking help to put their lives back in order. They were not casual or flippant about their sins or their confessions. They wanted to follow Christ. They hated what they had done. They struggled against their temptations, sought to find a way back, and desperately and humbly asked for help. Tragically, one of them gave up the fight.

HOW DOES GOD SEE SIN IN THE LIFE OF A BELIEVER?

God has provided abundant life through faith in Jesus Christ—and that abundant life includes ample victory over sin.

The Good News is better than most people believe. It is not only forgiveness for sin; there is much more! We can be freed from both the *penalty* and the *power* of sin. The Christian gospel is one of transformation, not just transaction. Scripture promises, "Sin will not be your master, because you are not under law but under God's grace" (Romans 6:14 NCV). God's grace has the power to keep us from sinning. God provides a way of escape from temptation so that we do not have to fall (1 Corinthians 10:13).

ON THE SURFACE OR DEEP IN THE HEART?

I hear people speak of salvation as though it were a business deal—a transaction rather than a transformation. In exchange for a moment of decision and a simple prayer, you are entitled to eternal life. Just say the magic words—*I accept you, Jesus, as my Savior*—and the deal is cut. Your sins are forgiven—past, present, and future—and you are now a child of God.

Once you've prayed that prayer and made that deal, you can pretty much do as you please. Don't let your religion interfere with your fun. If you sin, don't sweat it; you can always confess, and it's as if you had not done it. It's part of the deal you made. If you fall, you claim 1 John 1:9: "If we confess our sins, he will forgive us our sins."

This wonderful promise is both used and abused. It brings us reassurance when we are deeply convicted of sin and truly repent of the wrong we have done. There are times, though, when confession is made superficially, maybe even flippantly—*Oops, God, sorry 'bout that.* The trouble with that casual approach is that neither God nor the offender is fooled. We can only know and feel we are forgiven when our repentance is real.

HANGING OVER HELL

At the other extreme is a much tougher approach: To make sure you acquire the proper fear of God, some leaders hold you over the brink of hell until you nearly despair. You are shown your sins in detail along with your deserved destination. You are told that you are a helpless sinner of no value. If, however, you humbly identify yourself as scum, you are shown the way of escape through rigorous repentance. Then you are kept in the fold by reminders of how unworthy you are, how demanding God is, and what grave danger you face if you sin again. This sounds more like the Pharisees who were ready to stone the woman Jesus forgave.

BIBLICAL BALANCE

The examples above are extreme but not uncommon. Between the extremes lies what I think is a more balanced view taken from the book of 1 John:

1. **NO ONE IS EXEMPT FROM THE POSSIBILITY OF SINNING (1:8).**
2. **IT IS NEVER GOD'S WILL FOR US TO SIN (2:1).**
3. **SIN IS AN INTRUDER—NOT AN INVITED RESIDENT IN THE CHRISTIAN'S LIFE (3:6).**
4. **IF WE CLAIM TO NOT SIN BUT DO NOT OBEY THE TRUTH, WE FOOL OURSELVES (1:8).**
5. **IF WE GO ON WILLFULLY PRACTICING SIN, WE ARE NOT SAVED (3:6).**
6. **WE MAY STUMBLE OR STRUGGLE WITH COMPULSIVE BEHAVIOR BUT NOT DELIBERATELY LIVE A SINFUL LIFE (3:9).**
7. **IF WE SIN, JESUS REPRESENTS US TO THE FATHER,**

**SO THAT—THROUGH REPENTANCE AND FAITH—WE MAY
CONTINUE TO RECEIVE HIS GRACE AND WALK IN HIS
FELLOWSHIP (2:1-2).**

8. **IF WE REPENT AND CONFESS OUR SINS, GOD FORGIVES
   AND CLEANSES US (1:9).**

Paul brings up an issue in his letter to the Romans: "So do you think we should continue sinning so that God will give us even more grace? No! We died to our old sinful lives, so how can we continue living with sin?" (Romans 6:1–2 NCV).

Not only does God's grace (unmerited favor and empowerment) provide forgiveness for our weaknesses, there is mercy for compulsive wrong behavior. Even deliberate sinful choices can be fully forgiven. The method: "If we confess our sins, he will forgive our sins, because we can trust God to do what is right. He will cleanse us from all the wrongs we have done" (1 John 1:9 NCV).

BE SPECIFIC!

Pastor T. A. Hegre was my teacher and pastor for many years. An observant traveler, he told simple stories to illustrate truth. One story reminded us that the confession of sin must always be specific, never generalized.

In India he saw women washing their clothes by soaking them in the river and beating them on rocks. As he watched, a friend told him about a woman who once let her clothes remain soiled for so long that she was embarrassed to open her bundle in front of the other women, for they would see how dirty the garments were. To avoid exposure, she immersed the whole bundle in the water and then beat it on the rocks. Her clothes shook around a bit but did not get clean.

Pastor Hegre reminded us that sins are committed one by one and should be confessed one by one. When we sincerely confess and forsake our sins, God cleanses us.

To confess is to agree with God about the rightness or wrongness of what we have thought or said or done or failed to do. When we know we are wrong, we must admit our guilt. Remember these words of scripture: "If you hide your sins, you will not succeed. If you confess and reject them [or forsake them], you will receive mercy" (Proverbs 28:13 NCV).

VICTORY, YES!
SINLESS PERFECTION, NO!

Quite frankly, I have never heard anyone teach the idea of sinless perfection. Still, there are Christians who are more afraid of this holiness concept than of the idea that we can never experience victory.

Like millions of Christians, I accept what scripture proclaims: "The blood of Jesus Christ His Son cleanses us from all sin" (1 John 1:7 NKJV). "Sin will not be your master, because you are not under law, but under grace" (Romans 6:14).

There is no sin too dirty or too deeply rooted in our hearts for God to cleanse and remove. But the issue is not whether we will ever stumble into another sin; the issue is: Will we daily yield our lives to Christ and allow Him to make us the Christians that God wants us to be? Will we be clean, victorious, fruitful, and Spirit-filled?

When we look to Him and live for Him, we find the faith to believe that our sins are dealt with by the ever-available grace of God. We need to make sure that we love God and hate evil, that our repentance is complete, and that our trust in God is strong. God's forgiveness is big enough to handle any sin.

" 'WHO TOLD YOU
THAT YOU
WERE NAKED?' "

GENESIS 3:11

DO YOU REALLY
THINK IT'S CONCEALED?

WHEN OUR DAUGHTER MARCI was three years old, she took a daily afternoon nap. This was usually a carefree, happy time for her. She would lie in bed singing Sunday school songs before dropping off to sleep. Dolly worked busily around the house and was always content to hear Marci singing. One afternoon, however, Marci didn't sing.

For Dolly, Marci's silence seemed louder than her songs, and after awhile Dolly checked in to see what was happening. To her surprise, she saw Bible pages pasted on the wall from one side of the room to the other.

Why this sudden interest in displaying God's Word? Marci had gotten out her coloring crayons to draw pictures on the wall. Then she realized that Mommy wasn't going to like this, so she tore out several pages of her brother's Bible and carefully pasted them over the colorful drawings. She hoped she would be safe—after all, her deeds were covered with the Word of God! When Dolly entered the room, Marci discovered an important Bible principle:

"He who conceals his sins does not prosper, but whoever confesses and renounces them finds mercy" (PROVERBS 28:13).

As you might suspect, we have told this story more times than Marci would like to hear and have laughed at the foolishness of her childish attempts to hide her transgression. She did apologize, and she did find mercy.

ADULT COVER-UPS

How foolish children can be in their attempts to hide their wrongdoing—but their foolishness does not compare with the excuses that are made, the blaming that is done, and the cover-ups that are attempted by adults.

These attempts go back right to Eden where Adam and Eve disobeyed God's command in Genesis 3:6–12:

....

"When the woman saw that the fruit of the tree was good for food and pleasing to the eye, and also desirable for gaining wisdom, she took some and ate it. She also gave some to her husband, who was with her, and he ate it.

Then the eyes of both of them were opened, and they realized they were naked; so they sewed fig leaves together and made coverings for themselves.

Then the man and his wife heard the sound of the LORD God as he was walking in the garden in the cool of the day, and they hid from the LORD God among the trees of the garden. But the LORD God called to the man, 'Where are you?'

He answered, 'I heard you in the garden, and I was afraid because I was naked; so I hid.'

And he said, 'Who told you that you were naked? Have you eaten from the tree that I commanded you not to eat from?'

The man said, 'The woman you put here with me—she gave me some fruit from the tree, and I ate it.'"

....

THE SHAME AND BLAME GAME

We have all done it—rationalized, justified, excused, disguised, hidden, and called our errors by another name, or we have blamed other people. We may think that the worst thing that could possibly happen is to be exposed for who we are and what we have done.

When politicians are caught in transgressions, they may admit that they made some "bad choices" but hasten to assure us that their choices don't really reflect who they are.

Jesus, of course, would disagree.

....

"What comes out of a man is what makes him 'unclean.' For from within, out of men's hearts, come evil thoughts, sexual immorality, theft, murder, adultery, greed, malice, deceit, lewdness, envy, slander, arrogance and folly. All these evils come from inside and make a man 'unclean' " (MARK 7:20–23).

" 'No good tree bears bad fruit, nor does a bad tree bear good fruit' " (LUKE 6:43).

....

Adam and Eve didn't need to learn the technique from predecessors. It came naturally to them. It comes naturally to us. We want people to think well of us. We want to think well of ourselves. We protect our reputation even from the inner voice of conscience and especially from the searching of the Holy Spirit.

One of the most shameful stories in scripture describes the stupidity and cruelty practiced by King David, who was

described in Acts 13:22 as "a man after God's own heart." Read along from 2 Samuel 11:1–27:

"In the spring, at the time when kings go off to war, David sent Joab out with the king's men.... But David remained in Jerusalem.

One evening David got up from his bed and walked around on the roof of the palace. From the roof he saw a woman bathing. The woman was very beautiful, and David sent someone to find out about her. The man said, 'Isn't this Bathsheba, the daughter of Eliam and the wife of Uriah the Hittite?' Then David sent messengers to get her. She came to him, and he slept with her.... Then she went back home. The woman conceived and sent word to David, saying, 'I am pregnant.'

So David sent this word to Joab: 'Send me Uriah the Hittite.' And Joab sent him to David. When Uriah came to him, David asked him how Joab was, how the soldiers were and how the war was going. Then David said to Uriah, 'Go down to your house and wash your feet.' So Uriah left the palace, and a gift from the king was sent after him. But Uriah slept at the entrance to the palace with all his master's servants and did not go down to his house.

When David was told, 'Uriah did not go home,' he asked him, 'Haven't you just come from a distance? Why didn't you go home?'

Uriah said to David, 'The ark and Israel and Judah are staying in tents, and my master Joab and my lord's men are camped in the open fields. How could I go to my house to eat and drink and lie with my wife? As surely as you live, I will not do such a thing!'

Then David said to him, 'Stay here one more day, and tomorrow I will send you back.' So Uriah remained in Jerusalem that day and the next. At David's invitation, he ate and drank with him, and David made him drunk. But in the evening Uriah went out to sleep on his mat among his master's servants; he did not go home.

In the morning David wrote a letter to Joab and sent it with Uriah. In it he wrote, 'Put Uriah in the front line where the fighting is fiercest. Then withdraw from him so he will be struck down and die.'

So while Joab had the city under siege, he put Uriah at a place where he knew the strongest defenders were. When the men of the city came out and fought against Joab, some of the men in David's army fell; moreover, Uriah the Hittite died.

Joab sent David a full account of the battle. He instructed the messenger: 'When you have finished giving the king this account of the battle, the king's anger may flare up, and he may ask you, "Why did you get so close to the city to fight? Didn't you know they would shoot arrows from the wall? Who killed Abimelech son of Jerub-Besheth? Didn't a woman throw an upper millstone on him from the wall, so that he died in Thebez? Why did you get so close to the wall?" If he asks you this, then say to him, "Also, your servant Uriah the Hittite is dead...."'

David told the messenger, 'Say this to Joab: "Don't let this upset you; the sword devours one as well as another. Press the attack against the city and destroy it." Say this to encourage Joab.'

When Uriah's wife heard that her husband was dead, she mourned for him. After the time of mourning was over, David had her brought to his house, and she became his wife and bore him a son. But the thing David had done displeased the Lord.

....

THE BLESSING OF GETTING CAUGHT

Sure, David kept his sin from the public for a while, but he could not hide from the voice of his conscience. Nor could he hide from the voice of God. His sin caught up with him when the prophet Nathan came and told him what is now a well-known story: A wealthy man had many sheep but took the pet sheep of a poor shepherd who had only one, killed it, and served it to a traveler for dinner (2 Samuel 12:1–4).

Scripture records David's reaction to the story:

"David burned with anger against the man and said to Nathan, 'As surely as the LORD lives, the man who did this deserves to die! He must pay for that lamb four times over, because he did such a thing and had no pity' " (2 SAMUEL 12:5–6).

How righteous David sounds. He sympathizes with the poor shepherd and condemns the offender—until the faithful prophet points his finger at David and says in verse 7, "You are the man!" Until that moment, David felt that to be discovered was the worst thing that could happen to him. After all, both of his crimes were punishable by death in Israel. However, despite the danger, being caught was the best thing that could happen to David. He later rejoiced in Psalm 32:1–7 in the clean break he was able to make once he was caught:

"Blessed is he whose transgressions are forgiven, whose sins are covered. Blessed is the man whose sin the LORD does not count

against him and in whose spirit is no deceit.

When I kept silent, my bones wasted away through my groaning all day long. For day and night your hand was heavy upon me; my strength was sapped as in the heat of summer. Selah.

Then I acknowledged my sin to you and did not cover up my iniquity. I said, 'I will confess my transgressions to the LORD'— and you forgave the guilt of my sin. Selah.

Therefore let everyone who is godly pray to you while you may be found; surely when the mighty waters rise, they will not reach him.

You are my hiding place; you will protect me from trouble and surround me with songs of deliverance. Selah."

Yes, David, suffered for his sin in many ways including through the death of the child, but—once he came clean—the gnawing voice of his troubled conscience was silenced. His time of dryness was over, and his strength was renewed. Later, instead of hiding his faults, David would pray in Psalm 139:23–24:

"Search me, O God, and know my heart; test me and know my anxious thoughts. See if there is any offensive way in me, and lead me in the way everlasting."

GAINING A BIBLICAL
PERSPECTIVE ON CONSCIENCE

What is conscience? It's most commonly seen as the sense of what is right or wrong in one's behavior or motives—an inner arbitrator that approves or disapproves of thoughts, deeds, and attitudes. In the Judeo-Christian tradition, it's the inner sense of whether one is pleasing God and living up to His standards. Although the word rarely appears in the Old Testament, it is sprinkled liberally throughout the New Testament.

When Paul appeared before the Jewish court, having been accused of corrupting the faith of the nation, he said, "My brothers, I have fulfilled my duty to God in all good conscience to this day" (Acts 23:1).

Later his case was taken to the Roman governor Felix, to whom he said, "I strive always to keep my conscience clear before God and man" (Acts 24:16).

Paul did not necessarily equate the voice of the conscience to the voice of the Holy Spirit. He once admitted, "My conscience is clear, but that does not make me innocent. It is the Lord who judges me" (1 Corinthians 4:4).

John described the conflict that can exist between the voice of conscience and the voice of God:

....

"This then is...how we set our hearts at rest in his presence whenever our hearts condemn us. For God is greater than our hearts, and he knows everything.... If our hearts do not condemn us, we have confidence before God and receive from him anything we ask, because we obey his commands and do what pleases him"

(1 JOHN 3:19–22).

....

Paul warned believers not to hurt those who are too sensitive: "When you sin against your brothers in this way and wound their weak conscience, you sin against Christ" (1 Corinthians 8:12).

The conscience, Paul inferred, is not the final answer, because we don't all think alike: "Why should my freedom be judged by another's conscience?" (1 Corinthians 10:29).

Still, it is important to take good care of the conscience. It is formed by the moral and ethical training we receive, and it must be followed.

Paul wrote to his younger disciple Timothy: "The goal of this command is love, which comes from a pure heart and a good conscience and a sincere faith" (1 Timothy 1:5).

He put this in stronger language and reemphasized it later in the same chapter:

> *"I give you this instruction...so that...you may fight the good fight, holding on to faith and a good conscience. Some have rejected these and so have shipwrecked their faith"*
> (1 TIMOTHY 1:18–19).

I have learned to value his words very highly.

AN UNFORGETTABLE LESSON

One of the most important lessons I learned during my college days was that Christians need to get their consciences clean and keep them clean. During a prayer retreat, I heard college men apologize to one another for wrong attitudes and words. That weekend I learned that no one has peace of heart and mind unless he or she keeps clear accounts with God and other people.

As I grew in my Christian life, I made a list of several people whom I had offended or wronged in my teenage years. One by one I apologized and made things right with them. Though there were many offenses and some were more serious than others, one offense that deeply troubled me was the way I had deceived a neighbor and good friend.

Lloyd had become a follower of Christ about the same time I did. When he heard that I was studying for the ministry, he began to help me in any way he could. He sent books and a few modest cash gifts, but most important in my mind was that whenever I came home on break from college, he loaned me his car.

Since I had owned a couple of cars by then, Lloyd assumed that I had a valid driver's license. I'm ashamed to admit that I did not. I should have had a license by then, and I should have told him that I didn't have one—but I remained silent. Fortunately for me, no problems occurred, even though I used his car several times.

But when I attempted to pray more effectively and become more intimate with God, I often thought about the way I had deceived Lloyd. It occurred to me that I should confess to him that I had used his car under false pretenses, but I rationalized that nothing had happened and that confessing would only destroy our friendship.

Finally it became so hard to pray that I negotiated with God. "I don't think I should tell him. But if you really want me to, bring us together in a way that is so obviously not prearranged that I will know that is what you want (as if I didn't already know).

Soon after that prayer a famous evangelist came to town, and I decided to attend his meeting. I made my way toward the front of the auditorium looking for an empty seat, but there seemed to be none available. Finally I walked along the front row until I saw one empty seat in the crowd—right beside Lloyd.

I felt a simultaneous rush of excitement and fear when Lloyd saw me and waved for me to sit with him. I knew God had me where He wanted me, and I knew that I couldn't hesitate. So I sat down and opened my heart to Lloyd, clearing my conscience and rediscovering an ease in prayer that I had not known for some time. I also acquired an enormous motivation to be honest in my dealings with people, a lesson that has served me well.

That it's not easy to apologize is clearly stated in a short article by my friend LeRoy Dugan[1]:

THE WAY OF THE CROSS IN THREE SENTENCES

There are simple sentences that we hate to say:

I was wrong. We don't mind saying, "I might not have been totally correct," or "Maybe that wasn't the best thing to do." But "I was wrong" is the confession we need to make.

I'm sorry. It's no good to recognize guilt if we don't express sorrow and repentance.

Please forgive me. This requires humility. We cannot assume a posture of superiority when we ask forgiveness.

Three sentences—why do we avoid them? Often it's because of three deceptive ideas:

1. THE OTHER PERSON SHOULD MAKE THE FIRST MOVE.

2. IF I REPENT AND HE DOESN'T, THE SITUATION WON'T CHANGE.

3. IF I HUMBLE MYSELF, HE WILL FEEL CERTAIN HE IS RIGHT.

If you are living with one or more of these ideas, may I remind you of three facts:

1. JESUS KNEW THAT WE WERE ENTIRELY TO BLAME, BUT HE MADE THE FIRST MOVE TOWARD US.

2. JESUS WAS BAPTIZED AS THOUGH HE WAS A COMMON SINNER, WITH NO DEMANDS THAT ONLOOKERS DO THE SAME.

3. JESUS HUMBLED HIMSELF AND WAS OBEDIENT UNTO DEATH.

So I ask you, why shouldn't we go the way of the cross?

WHAT KINDS OF THINGS SHOULD WE MAKE RIGHT?

Some time ago I shortened and adapted the following list of questions from a Web site published by author and speaker Winkie Pratney. (You can read more about Winkie at winkiepratney.com.) This list is not meant to make you overly introspective but should instead help you to be objective in making your heart right with God and finding the peace that comes from having a clear conscience.

STEALING—Have you taken money or property that was not yours?

CHEATING—Have you gotten things from someone unfairly or dishonestly?

LYING—Have you practiced deception for selfish reasons?

SLANDER—Have you talked critically about people behind their backs?

IMMORALITY—Have you failed to keep your body and mind pure?

ENVY—Have you criticized others and exalted yourself?

PRIDE—Have you projected an untrue image of yourself?

INGRATITUDE—Have you taken the help of other people for granted?

ANGER—Have you shown impatience with someone?

CURSING—Have you used vulgar language with someone?

HABITS—Are you a slave to food, drink, or stimulants?

LAZINESS—Have you shirked your share of responsibility?

HINDRANCE—Have you prevented others from doing God's work?

HYPOCRISY—Has your falseness discouraged others from serving God?

BROKEN VOWS—Have you made vows to God and not kept them? (If it was an unwise vow, ask for forgiveness and release.)

WALK IN THE LIGHT

Drop your self-deceit. Face your sin and turn from it with all your heart. Decide that with God's help you will never return to your error again. Confession is humbling yourself and admitting you're wrong. Restitution is preparing to pay back or restore wherever possible.

Once you have received forgiveness from the Lord, ask Him for the courage and the wisdom to confess and restore to others whom you have wronged.

Your conscience must be clean before both God and man if you want to know peace of heart and true freedom. You do not have to confess every sin you have committed to everyone you know; but you should confess to individuals the specific sins you have committed against them. When you have cleared your conscience before God and man, you can trust God to fully restore your peace of heart and mind.

" 'YOU INTENDED
TO HARM ME,
BUT GOD INTENDED
IT FOR GOOD.' "

GENESIS 50:20

THEY PLOTTED EVIL!

EXTRAORDINARY AND INSPIRING EXAMPLES
of forgiveness are recorded in the Bible.

When Jesus said, " 'Father, forgive them, for they do not
know what they are doing' " in Luke 23:34, he set the standard
and the example for all of us to follow.

Steven, the first Christian martyr, took this example to heart
when he faced religious leaders and accused them of betraying
and murdering Jesus. They became furious and stoned him
to death. With his final breath Stephen prayed, " 'Lord Jesus,
receive my spirit,' " and " 'Lord, do not hold this sin against
them' " (Acts 7:59–60).

A third impressive biblical model is found in the life of

Joseph, the eleventh son of Jacob and the first born to Jacob's beloved wife, Rachel. Let's look into his story.

As a boy, Joseph was so much the favorite among Jacob's sons that his ten elder brothers became extremely angry and jealous of him. He was bright, protected, and had no sense of danger when he tattled to his father about the wrong things his brothers did.

They hated him for it.

Already a spoiled child in his home, Joseph was given a special multicolored robe that set him apart from the others. What really got to his brothers was the fact that Joseph was a dreamer and always the star performer in his own dreams! Could he keep those dreams to himself? Unfortunately for him, he could not. Every time he talked about them, he implied that his elder brothers would be his servants. Maybe he was the only one who understood the prophetic nature of those dreams, but he surely didn't know what to do with them.

When Joseph was about seventeen and his shepherd brothers were away tending the family flocks, Jacob sent him to see how they were doing. As he approached the grazing place, the brothers decided to kill him. Fortunately, two of the brothers decided they should not do that, but they were up against a strong majority. Reuben thought of a way to

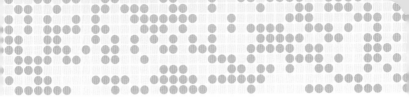

rescue him, but while he was gone for a short time, a group
of Ishmaelite traveling merchants who were headed for Egypt
appeared. Judah suggested they sell Joseph as a slave to these
merchants. The merchants, in turn, sold him to Potiphar, the
captain of the royal guard of Egypt.

JOSEPH HUMILIATED

Once in Potiphar's house, with the help of God, Joseph proved
to be an able administrator. Though he was a slave, he was such a
loyal person of integrity that Potiphar entrusted to him the care
of his entire household. He was admired by everybody, including
Potiphar's wife, who began to invite him to her bedroom for sex.
After he refused her invitations many times, she grabbed him and
desperately thrust herself upon him. He wisely ran from her room
and escaped her clutches—but unfortunately left his robe behind.

Angered by his refusal, she turned against him and accused him
of trying to rape her, resulting in Joseph's removal from the house
for imprisonment, where he spent the next thirteen years. Once
again his administrative skills were put to use in prison, and he
gained favor with the officials.

One has to wonder what went on in Joseph's mind. He was determined to be faithful to God and to a righteous way of life, but during the long, lonely nights, he must have wondered how his brothers and the others could do such things to him. Did he finally understand that his bragging had provoked the trouble? Did he decide to forgive his brothers for the sake of his love for his parents?

And then came the dreams again—not his this time, but the dreams of two fellow prisoners. God gave him the gift of interpreting their dreams accurately and describing their outcome. Later, Pharaoh had a dream that Joseph interpreted and, in addition, suggested a plan to save Egypt from a famine that was to come.

JOSEPH EXALTED

Joseph is the perfect example of the way God fulfills His word: "Humble yourselves, therefore, under God's mighty hand, that he may lift you up in due time" (1 Peter 5:6). Pharaoh saw in Joseph the qualities needed to administrate the coming times of prosperity and famine. Joseph became second-in-command in Egypt and even married Pharaoh's daughter, Asenath, with whom he had two sons. After so many years of suffering, Joseph finally had a peaceful, happy life.

The years of prosperity passed, and Joseph wisely stocked grain and other provisions to have on hand during the famine. Then, just as he had predicted, the drought came and the land dried up and produced no food. Egypt began to live off its surplus; they had enough to survive and even to sell to travelers who made their way to Egypt to buy from them.

In the midst of this famine extending to many nations including Canaan, Joseph's father, Jacob, heard that there was grain to buy in Egypt. When he could do nothing else, he sent his ten eldest sons to purchase grain, keeping only his youngest son, Benjamin, at home.

When the brothers arrived in Egypt, they were sent to Joseph to make their purchase—but they did not recognize the brother they had not seen in perhaps thirty years. Joseph, however, recognized them. What went through his mind?

He chose not to reveal himself and treated them a bit roughly, testing them to see if their hearts had changed. Had he forgiven them? It seems that he had but was not ready to speak out. He addressed them in the Egyptian language through an interpreter but listened carefully to their Hebrew conversations with each other.

Joseph demanded that they bring Benjamin back to prove that they were speaking the truth and then listened to what they

had to say to one another. Their conversation, recorded
in Genesis 42:21–22, softened his heart:

....

" 'Surely we are being punished because of our brother. We saw
how distressed he was when he pleaded with us for his life, but
we would not listen; that's why this distress has come upon us.'
    Reuben replied, 'Didn't I tell you not to sin against the boy?
But you wouldn't listen! Now we must give an accounting for
his blood.' "

....

They didn't know that Joseph understood and was moved by
every word they said. He decided to send them home, keeping
Simeon in custody while the rest went back to their father.

Finally their supplies ran out and they appeared in Egypt
again. This time Joseph created a situation in which
his brothers could be fully pardoned and empowered to
forgive themselves.

Finally, in Genesis 45:1–7, Joseph revealed who he was...

....

"Then Joseph could no longer control himself before all his
attendants, and he cried out, 'Have everyone leave my presence!'
So there was no one with Joseph when he made himself known
to his brothers. And he wept so loudly that the Egyptians heard

him, and Pharaoh's household heard about it.

Joseph said to his brothers, 'I am Joseph! Is my father still living?' But his brothers were not able to answer him, because they were terrified at his presence.

Then Joseph said to his brothers, 'Come close to me.' When they had done so, he said, 'I am your brother Joseph, the one you sold into Egypt! And now, do not be distressed and do not be angry with yourselves for selling me here, because it was to save lives that God sent me ahead of you. For two years now there has been famine in the land, and for the next five years there will not be plowing and reaping. But God sent me ahead of you to preserve for you a remnant on earth and to save your lives by a great deliverance.' "

JOSEPH THE PROVIDER

By now Joseph could put everything into perspective and see that God had allowed everything to happen in order to save a nation and Joseph's family. He called for his father to come and spend his last years in Egypt.

Back in Canaan, when the brothers gave their report, Jacob was overjoyed that the son whom he thought was dead was not only alive but calling for him. The whole family accepted Joseph's invitation and lived in peace and plenty in Egypt until Jacob died.

But Jacob's death brought up another tense moment. The brothers wondered if the absence of their father would change Joseph's mind about the forgiveness he had offered them. They thought they should strengthen their position:

....

" 'What if Joseph holds a grudge against us and pays us back for all the wrongs we did to him?' So they sent word to Joseph, saying, 'Your father left these instructions before he died: "This is what you are to say to Joseph: I ask you to forgive your brothers the sins and the wrongs they committed in treating you so badly." Now please forgive the sins of the servants of the God of your father.'

When their message came to him, Joseph wept.

His brothers then came and threw themselves down before him. 'We are your slaves,' they said.

But Joseph said to them, 'Don't be afraid. Am I in the place of God? You intended to harm me, but God intended it for good to accomplish what is now being done, the saving of many lives. So then, don't be afraid. I will provide for you and your children.' And he reassured them and spoke kindly to them"

(GENESIS 50:15–19).

....

YOU INTENDED TO HARM ME.
GOD INTENDED IT FOR GOOD!

The ten brothers were obviously culpable for what they did
to the gifted but spoiled Joseph. There was no excuse for their
cruelty. The punishment they exacted upon him did not fit
Joseph's "crime."

We admire Joseph because he was talented, kept himself pure
from the advances of Potiphar's wife, had spiritual perception
beyond the norm, was a capable administrator and a man of
integrity, *but he was not faultless!* In his early days, he was dreamy,
ambitious, and arrogant—negative qualities that would have to be
dealt with for him to become the man God wanted him to be.

He had to be taken down a notch or two, and he was.
"Humble yourself and God will exalt you" from 1 Peter 5:6 is
a spiritual principle to be honored. As God prepared Joseph to
save entire nations, including His chosen people and Joseph's
own family, the young man who was too enamored with himself
to be humble needed to be brought down so God could exalt
him. His brothers were part of that process.

Our generation has seen haughty spiritual leaders who
would have done well to learn the same lessons Joseph
experienced. The opposite of the humility-to-exaltation
principle is also true:

"Pride goes before destruction, a haughty spirit before a fall"
(PROVERBS 16:18).

"For whoever exalts himself will be humbled, and whoever humbles himself will be exalted" (MATTHEW 23:12).

We can thank God that he has a plan for our lives and that He works in us to prepare us for that plan. He also works in the world around us to prepare His plan for us:

"For we are God's workmanship, created in Christ Jesus to do good works, which God prepared in advance for us to do"
(EPHESIANS 2:10).

Joseph moved from pride to self-pity to shame to bitterness and then to humility and forgiveness. Joseph became the man God wanted him to be, the man who could be exalted and not glory in his exaltation. Joseph trusted in God and became the man in whom God could trust.

GOD KNOWS OUR HEARTS; WE HAVE ONLY OUR SUSPICIONS

How well do you handle humiliation, loss of position,

loss of recognition, and loss of significance? My greatest
fear in the ministry has always been that I would somehow
disqualify myself from fulfilling God's plan for my life.
I have prayed many times to be disciplined and pruned
rather than discarded.

A few years ago I began praying what I now call my default
prayer: "Help me to make my heart entirely Yours." I did not plan
to pray in this way; I just began doing it spontaneously several
times each day. It was at a time when things around me were
dramatically changing.

When the organization I worked with restructured and took
me out of the decision-making process, it hurt! When the church
I attended experienced sweeping changes—many of which were
negative, in my estimation—I spoke out. Although others felt the
way I did, they didn't speak up, and I felt I had to become
their voice.

I often stood alone in opposition to changes. I made
suggestions that did not gain acceptance. I thought that my fear of
disqualification was about to be realized.

Dolly and I felt like outsiders looking in. I spent many sleepless nights mulling over all the things I would like to say to certain people and what I thought they would probably say to me. Most of it was better left unsaid. Finally I resigned from the elders' board and we began attending another church. It was a low time in my life.

PRUNING AND DISCIPLINE

Then one Sunday morning we attended a Bible class led by my friend David. Seated in a circle, we were taking turns reading a passage from Bruce Wilkinson's book *Secrets of the Vine,* when we came to a passage where Wilkinson related what he had learned about pruning a grapevine in order to produce more fruit:

"The vine's ability to produce fruit increases each year, but without intensive pruning the plant weakens and its crop diminishes. Mature branches must be pruned hard to achieve maximum yields."[1]

Suddenly I knew what was happening with me. First, God was pruning things from my life so I could narrow my focus and concentrate only on things he had called and gifted me to do. Second, I realized that God was answering my prayer to make my heart totally His.

He was taking away the things that had become too important to me, and He was freeing me to love Him the way I wanted and needed to. Once I saw this and looked forward (by hope and by prayer) to greater fruit-bearing, I began to thank Him for the losses I had suffered and the lessons I had learned.

I then understood that when we sincerely pray for God to help us make our heart entirely His, He may work in ways that we do not expect or like. He may take away things that are too important—things that we have allowed to compete with Him for our affection and loyalty. If our hearts are to be well-tended and undivided, we may see that God is breaking down idols and limiting sources of pleasure.

Today I can see it all clearly. I have a new perspective on the happenings and a new outlook on life. I no longer blame certain people for the changes. I have forgiven them and moved on. We are friends again, and I understand that God used them in my life. I do not say that they intended anything for evil, but I do know that—in my life—God intended it for good.

I would not like to go through the trials again, but I can't bear the thought of going without the lessons I have learned.

" 'SON, YOUR SINS ARE FORGIVEN.' "

MARK 2:5

A FORGIVENESS
WE CAN LIVE WITH

TO FORGIVE THOSE WHO INJURE US must be tremendously important. I say that (1) because God calls us to it and (2) because it can be so hard to do! It may be doubly hard due to the wounds we suffer and the misconceptions we bring to the experience. If we think, for instance, that to forgive is simply to say, "All is forgiven and forgotten and things are as they were before," we are probably headed for some confusing and conflicting times.

We are complex human beings. Our memories are not easily erased. Our emotions are not immediately healed. Our thoughts, memories, and feelings become inner battlefields. Some offenses seem too wrong. Some pain seems too deep.

How can we forget the unforgettable? How can we forgive the unforgivable? How can we live with ourselves if we feel we have not forgiven as we know we should?

FOUR THINGS TO THINK ABOUT AS YOU PREPARE TO FORGIVE

BLESSINGS—Think of the peace and the freedom and the blessings you will enjoy once you commit to forgiving and making that forgiveness permanent. Ask yourself: Do I want to feel good again?

CONSEQUENCES—You may also need to contemplate the consequences of *not* forgiving. How long do you wish to prolong the feelings of resentment, guilt, and worthlessness?

ENABLING—You can be sure that if you accept the challenge of forgiving, you can pray and expect to be empowered by the Holy Spirit to be able to forgive.

MERCY—In the process of accepting God's forgiveness and extending mercy to offenders, you can also learn to be merciful to yourself.

STEPS TO FORGIVENESS

You and I are not the worst persons in the world simply because we are unable to feel jovial and magnanimous toward the people who have hurt us. The pain and resentment we feel after suffering a betrayal or an aggression are normal. Most people live with a certain amount of it. What many people do not experience is the freedom the Lord Jesus Christ provides when we ask Him to forgive us and empower us to forgive others.

Because the need for forgiveness is so common, there are many resources available to help us understand the process. One of my favorite books on the subject is *Total Forgiveness* by R. T. Kendall. A master preacher and former pastor of Westminster Chapel in London, Kendall combines his own experience along with theological and psychological research to offer us a powerful and instructive book.

Another excellent book is *Forgiving and Reconciling* by Everett L. Worthington Jr. Authored by an experienced counselor who had written previous works about forgiveness, this book tells how Worthington was subsequently forced to deal with his own reactions to the senseless and brutal murder of his mother by burglars.

My own research has not been nearly as extensive nor my counseling experience as broad as these two capable men, but I have studied forgiveness for several years and wrote a book that was published in Brazil in 1993 with the title *O Poder Restaurador do Perdão* (translated *The Healing Power of Forgiveness*).

Although we have never met, what the three of us have

in common is that each of us had our theories put to the test to see if we were willing to practice what we preached. I had written, "Forgive completely, unconditionally, generously, verbally, volitionally, and constantly."[1] I don't think I will ever forget asking myself if I could offer the forgiveness I had written about—or if I even wanted to. Kendall's book blessed me when I read it while on a mission trip to Kosovo. It helped me commit to following through on the forgiveness that I knew I should not withhold.

TAKING THE PLUNGE

Most of the literature about forgiveness includes instructions that in one form or another affirm the following helpful steps in the forgiveness experience. I have already mentioned these steps, some of them several times. In my experience and in the experience of many, these are liberating truths that restore spiritual and emotional health. They bear repeating. Don't take them as a formula, but see them as lessons that have come distilled through the lives of people like you and me who have been hurt and have had to learn to forgive.

1. DON'T BRUSH OFF THE OFFENSE. Unless it is a minor offense, we should not minimize the wrong that has been done, the mistake that has been committed, or the pain we have felt. Nor should we overlook, condone, or approve the wrong that has taken place. What's wrong is wrong. It is a mistake to shrug it off as though we were too tough or too mature to be affected by it. It is also wrong to suspect that we deserved it or it wouldn't have happened to us.

Obviously some small offenses can be shrugged off or taken in stride ("Be patient, bearing with one another in love," says Ephesians 4:2). These minor offenses may not be worth our time to process. But if the offense has been injurious to us or to our loved ones, we're better off admitting, "Yes, that hurt," before moving on. Even if we are able to see how God can use the offense or trial to increase our perseverance and godliness, we should not make light of the pain it caused. "Total forgiveness is achieved only when we acknowledge what was done without any denial or covering up—and still refuse to make the offender pay for his crime," says Kendall.[2]

2. PUT YOURSELF IN THE OFFENDER'S SHOES. Try to understand what prompted the person to do what he or she did. We may not be the best judges of this because we don't really know what has transpired in the other person's mind. Yet there is something healthy about attempting to understand what was going on in the other person's life that may have motivated him or her to do as he or she did. We have all had moments when we were not at our best. We have said or done things in the heat of emotion and while under stress that we now regret. Those who wounded us may have been at such a moment in their lives. We expect people to take those things into consideration when judging us, so let's be compassionate and forgive them as we expect them to do. "So in everything, do to others what you would have them do to you" (Matthew 7:12).

3. MAKE THE TOUGH DECISION THAT, WITH GOD'S HELP, YOU WILL FORGIVE. This means choosing not to retaliate, hate, reject, or get even with the person who hurt us. It also means that we are not going to speak negatively about the person or even think negatively. It means not using the person's offense as an excuse for our own attitudes of self-pity or acts of wrongdoing. It means giving up resentment and bitterness and hate. Resentment means to "feel again" the pain and disappointment we felt from the offense and the offenders. Too often we rethink, relive, and resent the happenings that took place. To forgive is to obey God and follow as closely as we can the example and standard laid down for us by our Savior, Jesus Christ. As long as we hold onto a grudge, we are allowing that person's actions to continue hurting us. Someone once said, "Holding a grudge

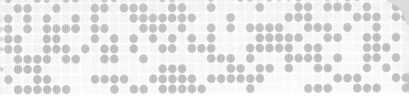

is like taking poison and waiting for the other person to die!"
Compare the words *forgive* and *forget*. Forgiving is a gift we get
from God and give to others. When we offer forgiveness to others
as an altruistic gift, it is more effective than when we forgive only
for our own benefit in an effort to "get over" the hurt.

4. TELL SOMEONE ABOUT IT. When I was betrayed by a
person I thought was a friend, telling someone—just one person—
would have helped me to clarify my thoughts and commit myself
to follow through. I don't mean that I needed to tell someone
what the person did (I have never done that and never will), but
I should have told someone that the person hurt me and that I was
committed to forgiving him. I would have known that someone
cared and was praying for me. Had I really forgiven? Yes, but when
the tempter—"the accuser of our brothers," as Satan is called in
Revelation 12:10—suggested that if I had truly forgiven, I wouldn't
feel as I did, it would have been nice to say, "Just ask my friend if I
have forgiven. He'll tell you that I did!" It can be extremely difficult
to be objective when our emotions are part of the equation. It's
helpful to bring a person into the picture to help us recover that
objectivity and sense of commitment.

When I first went to Brazil, I did not see eye to eye with a colleague, and we had several clashes. I have since learned that it's possible and even desirable to talk through disagreements, but we should limit the discussion to the issue at hand. We should not attack the person's character; instead, we should remain committed to the relationship with the person. In those days I did not have the understanding or maturity for that. We apologized to each other many times for our clashes.

Years went by, the colleague moved away, and I rarely saw him. One day while traveling with a mutual friend, I commented that I was happy that the colleague and I had patched things up and there was no longer a problem between us.

This mutual friend was surprised and said, "He doesn't see it that way. He thinks you still owe him an apology."

I was shocked. I searched my memory to see if I could think of an incident that I hadn't straightened out. I could think of no unturned ground. Later I asked for the Holy Spirit's guidance and came to the conclusion that the problem was not due to a specific incident but to the painful accumulation of offenses and to the fact that I had never acknowledged to him how deeply I had hurt him and how radically his life had been affected.

I sent off a letter detailing both of these issues and within a few days received an answer. I could tell that things had changed with him. He was not only receptive, but he also said that he was thankful and I was totally forgiven. It helped both of us to put it all to rest, get on with our lives, and enjoy a newfound freedom. We are now close friends. Our mutual friend did us both a service.

5. FOLLOW THROUGH. There is an act of forgiveness which may or may not be communicated to the offender, depending on the person's awareness of the offense. Then there is the process that follows. Once we are sure we have taken the first step of forgiveness, we embark on a commitment to not allow ourselves to relive the offense or resent the offender. It is very easy to slip. We think we deserve the right to feel sorry for ourselves, but once we turn down that road of self-pity, we need to do an immediate U-turn and change our thinking.

In one case, I forgave a person for something offensive, but I was in a setting where the subject came up frequently. Each time it did, I had to reaffirm the forgiveness I had offered. Jokingly I remarked, "Jesus said, 'Seventy times seven.' That makes 490. Right now I'm at 483!" Quite honestly, I voiced that forgiveness so many times that every time I heard the person's name, I would automatically declare, "He's forgiven!" He remains forgiven.

R. T. Kendall reproduced in his book a list of steps to forgiveness that he obtained from a secular source. They came out of a study group in Leeds, England, and were printed in the *Daily Express*[3]:

1. STOP EXCUSING, PARDONING, OR RATIONALIZING.

2. PINPOINT THE ACTIONS THAT HAVE HURT YOU.

3. SPEND TIME THINKING OF WAYS IN WHICH YOUR LIFE WOULD BE MORE SATISFYING IF YOU COULD EVER LET GO OF YOUR GRIEVANCES.

4. TRY REPLACING ANGRY THOUGHTS ABOUT THE "BADNESS" OF THE PERPETRATOR WITH THOUGHTS ABOUT HOW THE OFFENDER IS ALSO A HUMAN BEING WHO IS VULNERABLE TO HARM.

5. IDENTIFY WITH THE OFFENDER'S PROBABLE STATE OF MIND AT THE TIME OF THE OCCURRENCE. UNDERSTAND THE PERPETRATOR'S HISTORY WHILE NOT CONDONING HIS OR HER ACTIONS.

6. SPEND SOME TIME DEVELOPING GREATER COMPASSION TOWARDS THE PERPETRATOR.

7. BECOME MORE AWARE THAT YOU HAVE NEEDED OTHER PEOPLE'S FORGIVENESS IN THE PAST.

8. **MAKE A HEARTFELT RESOLUTION NOT TO PASS ON YOUR OWN PAIN.**

9. **SPEND TIME APPRECIATING THE SENSE OF PURPOSE AND DIRECTION THAT COMES AFTER STEPS 1-8.**

10. **ENJOY THE SENSE OF EMOTIONAL RELIEF THAT COMES WHEN THE BURDEN OF A GRUDGE HAS MELTED AWAY. ENJOY ALSO THE FEELING OF GOODWILL AND MERCY YOU HAVE SHOWN.**

Perhaps there is a name that affects you negatively. Maybe when you close your eyes you can see the face of an individual who has hurt you. Let me urge you to forgive and forgive and forgive again. Do not let the remembrance of their wrongdoing hurt you anymore. Do not allow yourself to think thoughts or say words that leave you feeling guilty in regard to that person. Let go of the pain. Forgive the person. Trust God for the grace to change your thoughts, words, and actions, and be free!

"BEAR WITH EACH OTHER AND FORGIVE WHATEVER GRIEVANCES YOU MAY HAVE AGAINST ONE ANOTHER. FORGIVE AS THE LORD FORGAVE YOU."

COLOSSIANS 3:13

IT CAN GET COMPLICATED

I STRUGGLED TO FOLLOW the agonizing narration of
Rhee, a Korean immigrant to Brazil, who appeared at my office
one day. He spoke broken Portuguese with a strong accent,
making communication difficult. I strained to get the details.

Rhee had come to Brazil to make a fortune, leaving his
wife behind with the promise, "I'll send for you when I can."
He never imagined that life would be so difficult in São Paulo.
Since he had no savings, he could not take time out to study
the Portuguese language. With no friends to open doors for
him, he worked at the most menial tasks, earning just enough
to stay alive. Seven years went by before he had saved enough
to send a ticket to his wife.

Back in Korea, she grew tired of waiting and began to see other men. By the time she arrived in Brazil, she was not the woman he had left behind. She was understandably angry and resentful, and she no longer loved him. She soon became interested in another man—and possibly more than one.

One day Rhee confronted the man she was seeing. They fought violently, and Rhee beat his adversary to death. Of course he was imprisoned for his crime. It could be observed that some people escape from prison and others escape to prison. That was the case with Rhee. Confined in São Paulo's "House of Detention," he heard the Christian gospel and surrendered his life to Jesus. He experienced forgiveness, and hope came to his heart. A weekly Christian group ministered to Rhee, and for the first time in many years he began to experience joy. Prison was a good experience for him, and he grew in the Lord.

When he was released, things changed. Back on the streets, he saw other Koreans prospering, but he remained poor and isolated. He tried to reconcile with his wife, but she wanted nothing to do with him. Left to himself, he became discouraged and bitter. Rhee convinced himself that his life had been destroyed by others and that the people who hurt him should in some way make retribution to him.

Besides that, he was terrified by the fear that the family and friends of the man he had killed would now want to murder him. Finally a ministry attempted to help him rebuild his life. They gave him work to do and a place to live. He submitted to the teachings and kept the rules, but he was not a happy man. Within the security of the Christian group he felt protected but dissatisfied and extremely restless.

I went to speak to the group, and just a few days later, he showed up on my doorstep—over 400 miles away. Was I his last hope? I hoped not. I could not blame him for feeling victimized, but in reality he was being victimized by himself, his foolish plans, his violent temper, and his bitter heart. The longer he pursued this reasoning, the more he would feel the victim.

None of the options he proposed made sense. Even the church he had attended wanted nothing more to do with him. There would be no restitution or reconciliation. The only things he could do were forgive those who had wronged him, put his unhappy past behind him, stand fast in the forgiveness he had received, and get on with his life. He was not prepared to do that.

FORGIVEN BUT UNABLE TO FORGIVE

Few of us have such a sad and tragic story to tell, but we all have a story. We have our heartaches, our regrets, and our bitter memories. We hold grudges. We seek revenge. Certain names, places, faces, and scenes produce negative reactions and remind us that we have problems to face and resolve. The person who is unable to forgive is often surprised by thoughts or feelings of anger, grief, and jealousy.

If we allow ourselves to dwell on thoughts like these, we run the risk of having a proverbial poisonous plant grow within us that will choke out our life and affect everyone around us spouses, children, grandchildren, and friends. We must not let that parasitic plant take root. Hebrews 12:14–15 exhorts us:

....

"Make every effort to live in peace with all men and to be holy; without holiness no one will see the Lord. See to it that no one misses the grace of God and that no bitter root grows up to cause trouble and defile many."

....

God is telling us…

LIVE IN PEACE.

BE HOLY.

DON'T MISS OUT ON GOD'S GRACE.

DON'T ALLOW BITTERNESS TO GROW.

DON'T SPREAD TROUBLE.

DON'T DEFILE OTHERS.

All around us, we see people who have lost their innocence and joy and have become bitter, unhappy individuals—but there is hope for them and for all of us.

HE'S WITH ME WHEREVER I GO!

A Christian came to my office to talk about his unhappy relationship with a person who was close to him. He said he felt very resentful toward him and was not willing to forgive him. He said he would prefer to never see the person again but confessed that he was completely dominated by the image of this person in his mind.

"He's with me wherever I go. When I go on a trip, he goes along. When I come home, he's waiting there for me. When I get up in the morning, he's the first person I see. When I lie down at night and close my eyes, I see him in the dark."

He wanted to get rid of this individual, but, ironically, the only way he could do it would be to forgive him, cancel his debt, and let it go. If he refused to do that, he might never find spiritual and emotional freedom.

A WAKE-UP AFFAIR

A man discovered that his wife was having an affair with a professor while taking a night course at the university. Even though he recognized that he had not invested in his own relationship with her as he should have and it was not what it ought to be, he still felt betrayed, hurt, and very jealous. The truth was, despite the deficiencies in their marriage, her affair woke him up and heightened his longing for her. As a result, he decided to consult a counselor to see if the marriage could be saved.

During one of his appointments, he confessed that he had deep feelings of hatred toward the professor and admitted that he had even dreamed of killing him. Although he was a Christian and a deacon in his church, he kept thinking of ways he could carry out an act of revenge.

When he began to understand the effects of his anger, he chose to forgive the man and direct charitable thoughts toward him and toward his wife. He was finally able to become free from his desire for revenge and to entrust the whole situation to God's care.

After a relatively short period of time, he felt God's powerful intervention restoring the marriage. After dealing with the suffering, the unfairness, the anger, and the sense of loss, he was ready to take his wife back and discover a new depth of relationship that he had not known before. Love and forgiveness had worked a miracle.

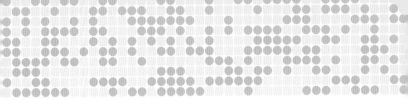

UNFORGIVABLE?

Forgiveness is a crucial part of any meaningful relationship.
We are all human and do things that hurt other people—
sometimes the people we love the most. We expect more from
them. When we get hurt, we often react by lashing out at
the person who hurt us. By forgiving, we are empowered
to move on without anger or hostility. If we hold on to those
things, we allow the act of aggression we have suffered to
continue hurting us.

What is an unforgivable act? A rape? A murder? A betrayal?
A kidnapping? A child molestation? Choosing to forgive the
perpetrator does not mean that we condone the act, nor does
it mean that we should remain passive or remain in a situation
where the person can hurt us again. We may forgive the person
and still approve of his incarceration. The purpose is not only to
punish the crime, but to protect society. Whatever the extenuating
circumstances, one fact remains: We must forgive!

Perhaps we should say that some acts are too difficult for
immediate forgiveness, but if we allow ourselves time to process
the information and the pain, we can eventually get to the

place where forgiveness is possible. Our first reaction may combine so much shock, pain, and anger that we are not able to forgive. We should take as much time as we need to work through our feelings.

MAKE NO UNREASONABLE DEMANDS OF YOURSELF

Still, the process will not begin until we decide to let it begin. Even though we may not feel like forgiving, the emotions will eventually follow the decision we make with our will and our intellect.

Do not place unreasonable demands upon yourself in the process of forgiving:

DO NOT THINK YOU MUST FEEL GOOD ABOUT THE SITUATION. You may never feel good about what happened, but you may begin to feel good about your forgiving response to it and about God's enabling grace.

DO NOT PLACE A DEMAND ON YOURSELF TO FORGET WHAT HAPPENED. Forgetting is not a choice we can make. Our memories, like our emotions, are involuntary responses. We may choose to remember by repeating and taking note of things, but we cannot choose to forget.

DO NOT FEEL OBLIGATED TO DEEPEN A RELATIONSHIP WITH THE PERSON WHO HURT YOU. In some cases it is advisable; in other cases it is not. You should not place yourself in harm's way. There were people whom Jesus rebuked and sent on their way without any attempt to reconnect.

DO NOT TRY TO DO IT ON YOUR OWN. Ask for and depend upon God's help to continue making the right choices and to receive the healing of your damaged emotions. You may also decide to enlist the help of a trusted friend or counselor to understand what's going on internally and to hold you to your commitment to forgive.

DO NOT USE THE PAST OFFENSE AS A LEVER OVER THE PERPETRATOR. The knowledge you have of a person's wrongdoing should not be passed on to others or used to pressure the individual.

DO NOT BE TOO HARD ON YOURSELF. No matter what you have done or what has been done to you, you are a person of value. Accept yourself as less than perfect but a unique and valuable creature of God's design.

DO NOT STAY DOWN. Do not allow your trauma to keep you distressed. Get up, get forgiven, get free, and get going again.

"FORGIVE AS THE LORD FORGAVE YOU."

COLOSSIANS 3:13

MAKE FORGIVENESS
WORK FOR YOU

SOME OF THE MOST USEFUL and widely circulated
material about forgiveness comes from the life and ministry
of Dutch author and speaker Corrie ten Boom (April 15,
1892–April 15, 1983). Known as a Holocaust survivor, her
story was made famous partially by a wonderful book cowritten
with John and Elizabeth Sherrill entitled *The Hiding Place*.

When the Nazi Third Reich of World War II stretched
its tentacles into Holland, the Jewish population was hunted
down and hauled away to prison camps, where they were
murdered as part of the well-known Holocaust atrocity.

The ten Boom family of Haarlem, Holland, committed the
"crime" against the Third Reich of hiding some of those Jews

in a secret place in their home located above the family watch shop. Many lives were saved, but eventually the Nazis arrested the ten Booms and incarcerated them in prison camps. The father died in one camp. Corrie and her sister Betsie were taken to the notorious women's camp at Ravensbrück, Germany, fifty miles north of Berlin. When the women were allowed to bathe, they had to remove their clothing and walk single file to the building where the showers were located, all while under the scrutiny of a dozen male guards. As they walked or stood in line, they were subjected to insults and lecherous looks from the prison guards.

Corrie related that Betsie was very pretty and had a delicate and attractive figure that attracted the attention of the guards. The lust on their faces and in their eyes was obvious. For Corrie, it was a humiliating and traumatic experience that left deep wounds in her soul. Betsie was constantly reminding Corrie that they needed to forgive the guards. Betsie later died in prison.

Despite all that Corrie suffered, she remained faithful to God and made a decision to forgive the Nazis. She promised God that after the war she would go wherever He wanted and take words of comfort to those who had suffered. Inwardly, she hoped that He would never call her to Germany. But, of course, He did. Here she tells what happens when she went to speak to a sad and distraught group of German believers:

LOVE YOUR ENEMY

"The solemn faces stared back at me, not quite daring to believe. There were never questions after a talk in Germany in 1947. People stood up in silence, in silence collected their wraps, in silence left the room.

"And that's when I saw him, working his way forward against the others. One moment I saw the overcoat and brown hat; the next, a blue uniform and a visored cap with its skull and crossbones. It came back with a rush: the huge room with its harsh overhead lights; the pathetic pile of dresses and shoes in the center of the floor; the shame of walking naked past this man. I could see my sister's frail form ahead of me, ribs sharp beneath the parchment skin. *Betsie, how thin you were!*

"The place was Ravensbrück and the man who was making his way forward had been a guard—one of the most cruel guards.

"Now he was in front of me, hand thrust out: 'A fine message, Fraulein! How good it is to know that, as you say, all our sins are at the bottom of the sea!'

"And I, who had spoken so glibly about forgiveness, fumbled in my pocketbook rather than take that hand. He would not remember me, of course—how could he remember one prisoner among those thousands of women?

"But I remembered him and the leather crop swinging from his belt. I was face-to-face with one of my captors, and my blood seemed to freeze.

" 'You mentioned Ravensbrück in your talk,' he was saying. 'I was a guard there.' No, he did not remember me.

" ' But since that time,' he went on, 'I have become a Christian. I know that God has forgiven me for the cruel things I did there, but I would like to hear it from your lips as well. Fraulein,'—again the hand came out—'will you forgive me?'

"And I stood there—I whose sins had again and again to be forgiven and could not forgive. Betsie had died in that place— could he erase her slow, terrible death simply for the asking?

"It could not have been many seconds that he stood there— hand held out—but to me it seemed hours as I wrestled with the most difficult thing I had ever had to do.

"For I had to do it—I knew that. The message that God forgives has a prior condition: that we forgive men those who have injured us. 'If you do not forgive men their trespasses,' Jesus says, 'neither will your Father in heaven forgive your trespasses.'

"I knew it not only as a commandment of God, but as a daily experience. Since the end of the war I had had a home in Holland for victims of Nazi brutality. Those who were able to forgive their former enemies were able also to return to the outside world and rebuild their lives, no matter what the physical scars. Those who nursed their bitterness remained invalids. It was as simple and as horrible as that.

"And still I stood there with the coldness clutching at my heart. But forgiveness is not an emotion—I knew that too. Forgiveness is an act of the will, and the will can function regardless of the temperature of the heart. 'Jesus, help me!' I prayed silently. 'I can lift my hand. I can do that much. You supply the feeling.'

"And so, woodenly, mechanically, I thrust my hand into the one stretched out to me. And as I did, an incredible thing took place. The current started in my shoulder, raced down my arm, sprang into our joined hands. And then this healing warmth seemed to flood my whole being, bringing tears to my eyes.

" 'I forgive you, brother!' I cried. 'With all my heart.'

"For a long moment we grasped each other's hands, the former guard and the former prisoner. I had never known God's love so intensely as I did then. But even so, I realized it was not my love. I had tried and did not have the power. It was the power of the Holy Spirit as recorded in Romans 5:5: '...Because the love of God is shed abroad in our hearts by the Holy Ghost which is given to us' " (KJV)[1].

MOVING ON

The experience of forgiveness does not end with the decision. No matter how great or small the emotional release, we have to follow through. If we allow ourselves to dwell on the details of the act we have forgiven, we may experience the resentment again. We may relive the experience to such a degree that the memory becomes as painful as it was when we first felt the injury.

Along with the pain may come a deep sense of frustration. We may think, "I already made the decision to forgive, but I guess it didn't work." Or we may hear that accusing voice of Satan saying, "If you had really forgiven, you wouldn't be feeling all this resentment now.

One problem is that our emotions do not always align with our choices. We made the decision because it was the right thing to do, but we still feel hurt. It is my observation that if we hold firmly to our decision to forgive and don't allow ourselves to dwell on the details of what hurt us, the emotions will eventually subside and align with our decision. Corrie ten Boom writes:

"Forgiveness is like letting go of a bell rope. If you have ever seen a country church with a bell in the steeple, you will remember that to get the bell ringing you have to tug awhile.

Once it has begun to ring, you merely maintain the momentum. As long as you keep pulling, the bell keeps ringing. Forgiveness is letting go of the rope. It is just that simple. But when you do so, the bell keeps ringing. Momentum is still at work. However, if you keep your hands off the rope, the bell will begin to slow and eventually stop."[2]

....

The offense starts the inner bell ringing. Every time we think about it, we are taking the rope in our hands and pulling it, causing the bell to ring another time. Then we make a decision to forgive and let go of the bell, but the bell of emotions keeps ringing. Momentum is created. The habit is formed. Every time we hear the bell ring, we tug at the rope again and prolong the ringing.

It is now time to let go of the rope. Even though the bell keeps ringing, if we choose not to pull at the memory, the ringing will grow softer and softer until it rings no more.

Our emotions make no decisions on their own. They follow the leading of our thoughts, words, and actions. If we refuse to dwell on it, we will find healing for our emotions and the pain will subside.

"THE LORD SAYS,
'FORGET WHAT
HAPPENED BEFORE.' "

ISAIAH 43:18 NCV

CAN I EVER FORGET?

"WELL, NOW, YOU JUST NEED to forgive and forget!" Really? A common misconception is that to forget offenses can only mean to have them completely wiped from our memory.

A more realistic view is that we can be so healed from our hurts that we can remember them without being haunted by them. We know exactly what happened, but we have forgiven and let the issues go to the extent that we now feel little or no pain.

The Random House Dictionary suggests four definitions for the word *forget*: (1) to cease or fail to remember, (2) to neglect intentionally, (3) to overlook or disregard, and (4) to cease or omit to think of something.

To forget in the healthy biblical sense is to choose not to dwell on the offense, to intentionally disregard it, to not think about it, and to not bring up the subject again or hold it against the offender.

"Forgive and forget" is a terrific motto to live by—if we understand what it means. It does not mean to repress a memory. That would be comparable to disregarding a nagging infection. Denial of its presence does not prevent the spread of destruction. The infection must be treated, and the infected areas must be healed.

Our loving heavenly Father does not want us to feel guilty about our inability to have spotless memories. We are not required to feel good about the offenses that have occurred. God is a God of truth, and He knows we must face the reality of our sufferings and then forgive. We may remember and still forgive, but if we free the offender, we ourselves are set free.

SELECTIVE MEMORY

David composed a fascinating prayer about God's memory in Psalm 25:6–7. The New Century Version says it this way:

"LORD, remember your mercy and love that you have shown since long ago. Do not remember the sins and wrong

things I did when I was young. But remember to love me always
because you are good, LORD."

....

David was not asking God to lose His memory but to be
selective with it—to remember mercy and love but to forget
the sins of his youth.

I think David understood that to forget does not mean to
catch amnesia concerning the offense. Rather, it means choosing
not to hold it against the offender. In this case, David knew his
sins were still registered in God's memory, but he asked God not
to bring them up again or hold them against him.

His prayer aligned with God's character because once we
have asked God to forgive our sins, He does not bring them
up again. It should be the same with us. We must decide not
to call up undesirable memories with the purpose of brooding
over them or feeding the hurts they once caused us. Healing can
actually enable us to reflect on the situations painlessly and draw
valuable lessons from them.

When Paul said he practiced "forgetting things behind" in
Philippians 3:13, he wasn't talking about leaving his socks in
hotel rooms, and I'm sure he wasn't describing a once-and-for-
all occurrence. He mentioned at least six times in the Bible that
he had persecuted Christians. His memory hadn't been erased,

but he had dealt with his past in the way that God prescribes, the way that frees us from pain. His statement in 1 Corinthians 15:9–10 NCV is amazing:

....

"All the other apostles are greater than I am. I am not even good enough to be called an apostle, because I persecuted the church of God. But God's grace has made me what I am, and his grace to me was not wasted. I worked harder than all the other apostles. (But it was not I really; it was God's grace that was with me.)"

....

Paul remembered what he had done and acknowledged that persecution of Christians had been part of his life, but he knew that God's grace was greater than all his sin—grace that forgave him, grace that enabled him to be effective. "Where sin increased, grace increased all the more" (Romans 5:20 NIV).

Like computer data, our past has been entered into our memory. We may see it pop up on the directory of our mind, but we do not have to download the file for review.

CHOOSING NOT TO REMEMBER

We have already mentioned the story of Joseph, one of history's most engaging stories of forgiveness.

Thirty years later Joseph had his chance for revenge, but he did not take it. Instead, he forgave them. When he finally revealed himself to his brothers, they feared for their lives. By then Joseph had gained understanding from the Lord and healing for his wounds. He was enabled by God to care for his brothers and treat them kindly. He hadn't forgotten what they had done, but he refused to hold it against them.

"YOU'LL NEVER LET ME FORGET"

Too often forgiveness is partial or even false. A true sign of forgiveness is that, once reconciliation has occurred, we do not bring up the offense again—except for mutually agreeable constructive purposes. When God forgives and "forgets" our sins, it means that He will never bring them up against us. We should do with the sins of others exactly what God does with ours.

IN THE ASHES

Let me refer once more to Corrie ten Boom. The following experience is taken from her book *Tramp for the Lord*:

"I recall the time...when some Christian friends whom I loved and trusted did something which hurt me.... Many years later, after I had passed my eightieth birthday, an American friend came to visit me in Holland. As we sat in my little apartment in Baarn, he asked me about those people from long ago who had taken advantage of me.

" 'It is nothing,' I said a little smugly. 'It is all forgiven.'

" 'By you, yes,' he said. 'But what about them? Have they accepted your forgiveness?'

" 'They say there is nothing to forgive! They deny it ever happened. No matter what they say, though, I can prove they were wrong.' I went eagerly to my desk. 'See, I have it in black and white! I saved all their letters and I can show you where...'

" 'Corrie!' My friend slipped his arm through mine and gently closed the drawer. 'Aren't you the one whose sins are at the bottom of the sea? Yet are the sins of your friends etched in black and white?'

"For an astonishing moment I could not find my voice. 'Lord Jesus,' I whispered at last, 'who takes all my sins away, forgive me for preserving all these years the evidence against others! Give me the grace to burn all the black and whites as a sweet-smelling sacrifice to your glory.'

"I did not go to sleep that night until I had gone through my desk and pulled out those letters—curling now with age—and fed them all into my little coal-burning grate. As the flames leaped and glowed, so did my heart. 'Forgive us our trespasses,'

Jesus taught us to pray, 'as we forgive those who trespass against us.' In the ashes of those letters I was seeing yet another facet of His mercy."[1]

Corrie took a fresh step of obedience that would help her to truly forgive and to forget in the most biblical sense of the word.

UNFINISHED BUSINESS

When our memory haunts us in the area of right or wrong, it's often because our conscience, prompted by the Holy Spirit, is reminding us of some error that we need to correct. It's only when we correct the error that the nagging voice is silenced and we find peace. If we have done everything we know to do and the feeling of condemnation persists, we may suspect that an evil spirit is accusing us in order to keep us discouraged. In that case we can follow the Bible's counsel of James 4:6–8 (NIV): " 'God opposes the proud but gives grace to the humble.' Submit yourselves, then, to God. Resist the devil, and he will flee from you. Come near to God and he will come near to you."

AS THOUGH IT WERE
HAPPENING FOR THE FIRST TIME

A story is told about a Christian who, in a certain area of his life, had been tempted constantly and had fallen occasionally into sin. Each time, he confessed his sin to God and asked forgiveness.

When he experienced another failure in that area, he said, "There I've gone and done it again. I'm sorry, Lord. Will you forgive me one more time?"

The Lord said, "Oh, had you done that before?"

God doesn't say, for instance, "Let's see, now, that's thirteen times you've hollered at your kids this month; how long do you think I'm going to keep forgiving you?"

Though He knows everything we have done, He treats each sin as though it were happening for the first time.

A GOD OF GRACE AND MERCY

At the core of who God is, we find a heart of compassion and mercy. His thoughts toward us are good. He longs to bless us and draw us into an increasingly satisfying relationship. He forgives, He forgets, He redeems, He transforms, and He blesses us. David expressed these ideas in Psalm 103:8–17 (NIV):

....

"The LORD is compassionate and gracious, slow to anger,
abounding in love. He will not always accuse, nor will he harbor
his anger forever; he does not treat us as our sins deserve or repay
us according to our iniquities. For as high as the heavens are
above the earth, so great is his love for those who
fear him; as far as the east is from the west, so far has he removed
our transgressions from us. As a father has compassion on his
children, so the LORD has compassion on those who fear him; for
he knows how we are formed, he remembers that we
are dust. As for man, his days are like grass, he flourishes like a
flower of the field; the wind blows over it and it is gone,
and its place remembers it no more.

But from everlasting to everlasting the LORD's love is
with those who fear him, and his righteousness with their
children's children."

....

The prophet Micah says, "You will again have compassion
on us; you will tread our sins underfoot and hurl all our
iniquities into the depths of the sea" (Micah 7:19 NIV).

To that Dwight L. Moody adds this note: "God has cast
our confessed sins into the depths of the sea, and He's even
put a 'NO FISHING' sign over the spot."

"I CAN'T
FORGET MY SIN."

PSALM 51:3 NCV

CAN I FORGIVE MYSELF?

"I CAN'T FORGIVE MYSELF. Even if God has forgiven me (and I hope He has), I will never be able to forget what I did or forgive myself."

What do people mean when they say that?

—I HAVE TOO MANY REGRETS.

—THINGS COULD HAVE BEEN DIFFERENT.

—I CAN'T BELIEVE I LET MYSELF DO THAT.

—I CAUSED TOO MUCH SUFFERING.

—I'M SO EMBARRASSED AND ASHAMED.

—I HAVEN'T SUFFERED ENOUGH FOR WHAT I DID.

—I NEED TO ATONE.

—I DON'T DESERVE TO BE HAPPY.

AT WHAT POINT DO
WE DESERVE FORGIVENESS?

I was surprised one day to hear a friend pray, "Thank you, Lord. You've been merciful to us, even though there have been times when we didn't deserve your mercy."

The moment wasn't right for a theological discussion, but I thought, *When has receiving mercy ever depended upon our deserving it?*

Let's start with the right supposition: As sinners (and we all are), none of us deserves forgiveness. If we deserved it, we wouldn't need it. Mercy comes to us because a merciful God never stops being merciful. God extends His mercy to undeserving people. God's merciful arms are always outstretched toward us.

Beyond that, forgiveness comes because God in His mercy provided His Son, our Lord and Savior Jesus Christ, to pay the debt of our sin. Our humble repentance and faith in Christ releases His forgiveness, which comes to us through Christ's worthiness—not our own. And it comes to us through Christ's suffering, not ours.

The reformer Martin Luther was appalled by the ways the priests of his time handled the sin and guilt of their people. To wealthy parishioners, priests sold special indulgences said

to provide escape from punishment for individuals and their relatives—dead or alive. To the poor they prescribed "penance"— a practice that sometimes included beating oneself with a whip. This was meant to help sinners feel worthy of forgiveness (or perhaps to encourage them to come up with the money to buy indulgences to pad the coffers of the church).

The practice has been eliminated from the church, but it lives on in many of our hearts. We berate ourselves and put ourselves through mental and emotional punishment with the hope of someday feeling worthy of forgiveness. Only after we have suffered enough do we feel it may be all right to enjoy life again. And maybe we think that we could never suffer enough.

WHAT CAN WASH AWAY MY SIN?

No punishment we suffer—self-inflicted or otherwise—can wash away wrongdoing. Sin is more serious than that. Only the blood that Jesus shed on Calvary's cross can cleanse away guilt. Only the blood of Jesus can bring peace to the anguished heart bent on revenge or self-destruction.

If suffering, sacrifice, or religious duty could make atonement for our sin, the value of our Lord Jesus Christ and His vicarious death for us would be greatly diminished. Our value would be greater than His. If our suffering and sacrifice could make us deserving of salvation, God the Father would have to apologize to Jesus for sending Him to suffer for us.

So the songwriter understood well when he wrote...

....

What can wash away my sin? Nothing but the blood of Jesus.
What can make me whole again? Nothing but the blood of Jesus.
Oh! Precious is the flow that makes me white as snow;
No other fount I know, nothing but the blood of Jesus.[1]

....

THE ONLY WAY

On a flight from Slovenia to Kosovo, I noticed that a flight attendant wore a tiny gold cross on a delicate gold chain, and it was fastened rather tightly around her neck.

"Does that mean you are a Christian?" I asked her as she served me.

She thought for a moment and answered, "Yes, I am a Christian, but I don't often go to church because I disagree with the many people there who say that Jesus is the 'only way.' "

She moved quickly to another passenger and our conversation ended.

As she went about her work, I thought to myself, *If the cross means anything, it means that Jesus is the only way, because why would the Father send His beloved Son Jesus to the cross to die if there was another way by which we could be saved?"*

But God has no apologies to make and no regrets concerning the sacrificial death of His Son. He has no hidden resentment toward us for causing Christ's suffering.

....

"For I know the thoughts that I think toward you, saith the LORD, thoughts of peace, and not of evil"
(JEREMIAH 29:11 KJV).

....

God wants us to be forgiven and free! He wants our happiness to be restored. Abundant life is offered to all regardless of what we have done. So, rather than maintain an attitude of self-hatred, rejection, worthlessness, and unforgiveness, we should decide to think, "I know I am unworthy to receive forgiveness, but if Christ died to provide it for me, how can I be so ungrateful as to reject it? And if He has fully forgiven me, why should I be so foolish as to not forgive myself?"

WHY SHOULD WE
FORGIVE OURSELVES?

To his brilliant book *Total Forgiveness,* R. T. Kendall has added another volume that I found equally illuminating: *How to Forgive Ourselves—Totally.* I was also pleased to find that his respected biblical scholarship confirmed in greater detail what I had written years ago in this book published first in Portuguese.

Kendall explains what he means by totally forgiving ourselves: "It is accepting God's forgiveness of all our past sins and failures so completely that we equally let ourselves off the hook for our pasts as God Himself has done. It also means that since I must forgive others totally, I must equally forgive myself totally."

He explains that many people feel guilty at the thought of totally forgiving themselves. "The idea is this," he says, "What I have done is so horrible that I do not deserve to be set free from guilt. It would be irresponsible to forgive myself totally and not look back. I must pay for my failure. I must see that I get justice."[2]

SHE FELT POLLUTED
AND ABNORMAL

I was speaking in a Brazilian church composed mostly of young Christians. The subject was self-acceptance. I based my talk on

David's affirmation in Psalm 139:14 NIV: "I praise you because I am fearfully and wonderfully made; your works are wonderful, I know that full well."

I asked the young people to consider that each of them was a unique character, created by God with gifts and abilities to fill a special role in life. I urged them to be thankful for the way God made them and to accept themselves as they were.

After the close of the meeting, a young woman shook my hand at the door and asked, "What if we can't accept ourselves, but it's not because of the way God made us?"

I could tell that her problem was not with her looks, as it is with so many people. She was a good-looking girl with a pretty face and trim figure. In fact, I could see that she could be prettier than she allowed herself to appear. She preferred the tomboy look. She seemed to be hiding her best attributes.

I asked, "Would you like to be more specific?"

She cowered a bit and said, "Mercy, no!"

"Would you like to talk?" I inquired.

"No," she said rather hesitantly and walked away.

I noticed that she didn't leave but sat down in front of the church on the curb. When almost everyone was gone, I went over and asked, "Are you sure you wouldn't like to talk?"

Reluctantly she said she would.

So we found a seat and she started telling her story. At first she circled a bit but finally said she had weird dreams that many times were sexual in nature, and she considered them perverted. She thought there must be something wrong with her to have those kinds of dreams. She felt polluted and abnormal.

She began weeping and finally admitted, "I have had sex with my three brothers." Her emotional intensity suggested that these were recent events.

"When did this happen?" I asked.

"Let's see," she said, "I'm twenty-one now, and it happened when I was twelve."

"And it's never happened again?" I inquired.

"Never again!" she insisted.

."Not with anyone?"

"No! I'm a Christian now and I would never do that. Besides, I think I'm a little abnormal!"

I insisted that she wasn't abnormal. "You've behaved properly for nine years. You are a normal person who has been hurt, and you have some deep scars that keep reappearing."

When I assured her that she was normal, she began to weep again. Could she allow herself to believe that?

I asked her to do the difficult thing she had never had the courage to do before—to talk with her three brothers and ask

for their forgiveness. (In reality, they should have asked her, but I had no access to them and she was a consenting partner.)

She went home determined to set things straight but almost lost courage. Finally she went to them one by one and said, "You remember what we did when we were younger? Please forgive me." Each of them responded in the same fashion: "Thank you for bringing it up, and please forgive me, too."

Having been forgiven by God and by her brothers, she was able to forgive herself and allow herself to be feminine again. Her lovely features reappeared, and the change was enormous.

THE PUREST OF VIRGINS

Sexual sins always seem to be cloaked in a special kind of shame—especially for women. Though God doesn't appear to see these acts—perverted as they may be—as worse than other sins, they have a way of leaving a mark upon us. It seems that many women find it especially difficult to regain their sense of worth after involvement in sexually immoral behavior.

Several years ago I spoke to the students of a Bible institute. During the sermon, I felt prompted to switch topics for a moment and say, "If there is a young girl here who has fallen into the sin of fornication but has repented of that sin, I want you to know that God sees you as the purest of virgins."

Later that day a young woman said, "Thank you, Pastor. Those words were for me. You'll never know how much they meant."

GO AND SIN NO MORE

A woman was dragged into the presence of Jesus to be judged for her sin of adultery. (In reality, it was Jesus who was being judged by the self-righteous, evil "lynch mob.") They reminded Jesus that Moses had determined that such women should be stoned and asked Him to state what His sentence would be. Jesus said to the mob, " 'If any one of you is without sin, let him be the first to throw a stone at her.' " After they had left, Jesus turned to the woman and said, " 'Woman, where are they? Has no one condemned you?' " She responded, " 'No one, sir.' " Jesus then looked at her and spoke words that have been repeated for centuries around the world: " 'Then neither do I condemn you.... Go now and leave your life of sin' " (see John 8:7–11).

I have no way of knowing for sure, but something tells me that the strength she received at that moment enabled her to leave her past behind her and live a transformed life from then on. That's what Jesus wants for all of us.

THE GREATER THE SIN,
THE GREATER THE LOVE

Another woman with a similar story felt such gratitude and love to Jesus for His forgiveness that she washed His feet with tears and perfume and wiped them dry with her hair.

The self-righteous Pharisees, who admitted no need (and perhaps no provision) for forgiveness, criticized the woman's extravagant and wasteful act. And they scorned her for her sinful past.

Jesus understood her perfectly and accepted her love and worship. He then told a story:

....

" 'Two people owed money to the same banker. One owed *five hundred coins and the other owed fifty. They had no money to pay what they owed, but the banker told both of them they did not have to pay him. Which person will love the banker more?' Simon, the Pharisee, answered, 'I think it would be the one who owed the most money.' Jesus said to Simon, 'You are right'.... Jesus said to the woman, 'Because you believed, you are saved from your sins. Go in peace.' "* (LUKE 7:41–43, 50 NCV).

....

WE CANNOT DIVORCE WHAT
WE DO FROM WHO WE ARE

Part of the difficulty with forgiving ourselves is that we have to identify what we have done and take responsibility for it. Our offense becomes part of our identity.

A young woman was found guilty and sentenced to five years in prison because, after having sex with a partner who then wanted nothing more to do with her, she obtained the help of a friend, tied the man up, and used a hot metal object to brand the letter *R* onto his abdomen, leaving a permanent scar. Her lawyer said, "She's a good kid—despite the picture painted of her—who exercised poor judgment and got herself into a bad situation. She is not the monster the prosecution made her out to be."

A candidate for political office had previously been a comedian and a writer. It was discovered that he had written an article in extremely bad taste for *Playboy Magazine*. His party officials excused his behavior, saying, "That was the comedian; this is the politician." Were they two different people? It's possible that he has repented, so I'll give him the benefit of the doubt, but I certainly wasn't convinced by the argument given by the party member. Was it excusable for the comedian but not the candidate? Were they not one and the same?

What we do is the result of the kind of people we are. We commit sins because we are sinful at heart. We need to be forgiven and transformed into people whose hearts are pure. We can pray as David did in Psalm 51:7: "Wash me, and I will be whiter than snow"!

GIVE ME JOY!

Should a Christian who has committed a terrible sin ever allow himself the luxurious feeling of joy? King David of Israel committed one of the most notorious sins recorded in the Bible. When he was faced with the double sins of adultery and murder, he prayed, "I know about my wrongs, and I can't forget my sin. You are the only one I have sinned against; I have done what you say is wrong. You are right when you speak and fair when you judge" (Psalm 51:3–4 NCV).

But once David had fully repented of his sin and accepted God's forgiveness, he did not think it was too much to ask, "Restore to me the joy of your salvation and grant me a willing spirit, to sustain me" (Psalm 51:12).

When you read Psalm 32:1 NCV, you understand how fully God answered David's prayer: "Happy is the person whose sins are forgiven, whose wrongs are pardoned."

Before his conversion to Christ, the apostle Paul was known as Saul, a persecutor of the Christian church. When Stephen became the first Christian martyr, stoned to death for his dedicatic to and defense of the gospel, Saul stood and watched: "And Saul was there, giving approval to his death" (Acts 8:1).

Paul could have been guilt-ridden for the rest of his days. Instead he lived by the words that he leaves as counsel for you and me in Philippians 3:13–14: "But one thing I do: Forgetting what is behind and straining toward what is ahead, I press on toward the goal to wi the prize for which God has called me heavenward in Christ Jesus."

WHERE CAN WE UNLOAD OUR GUILT?

David Seamands once pointed out in a sermon[3] that there are only three places we can deposit the guilt of our sins:

1. **ON THE CROSS, WHERE JESUS "CARRIED OUR SINS IN HIS BODY...AND [WE] ARE HEALED BECAUSE OF HIS WOUNDS" (1 PETER 2:24)**

2. **ON OURSELVES, WHERE THROUGH SELF-INFLICTED SUFFERING AND EMOTION-BASED SICKNESS WE TRY TO MAKE ATONEMENT FOR OUR WRONGDOINGS**

3. **ON OTHERS, USUALLY THE PEOPLE CLOSEST TO US, WHO BEAR THE MARKS OF OUR ANGER AND**

FRUSTRATION BY BECOMING SCAPEGOATS FOR
EVERYTHING WRONG THAT HAPPENS TO US.

The right place is obviously the cross. Should we forgive ourselves? Should we allow ourselves to feel fully forgiven? I suggest that...

—IF FORGIVENESS STEMS FROM GOD'S MERCIFUL
CHARACTER... (AND IT DOES!)
—IF FORGIVENESS IS AVAILABLE TO US THROUGH CHRIST'S
ATONEMENT... (AND IT IS!)
—IF GOD NO LONGER CONSIDERS US GUILTY...
(AND HE DOESN'T!)
—IF GOD NO LONGER REMEMBERS OUR SINS AGAINST US...
(AND HE DOESN'T!)
—IF GOD IS WORTHY OF OUR TRUST...
(HE IS INFINITELY WORTHY!)

Then, though we are less worthy than we can possibly imagine, we should consider ourselves truly forgiven—not through our worthiness, but His. Not by our suffering, but His. Not by what we can pay, but by what He has paid. If He can forgive us, then for His sake, for our sake, for everyone's sake, let us forgive ourselves.

" 'I DO BELIEVE.
HELP ME TO
BELIEVE MORE!' "

MARK 9:24

FORGIVING BY FAITH

ON SOME OCCASIONS, we may know that we are required to forgive but feel unable to do so. Forgiveness then demands a power that is greater than our own. By being willing to forgive, we have already taken the first step— but we need God's help to forgive freely and fully.

Help is available to all who ask for it and receive it by faith. Trusting in the power of the Spirit who indwells us and fills us, we can find the ability to love and forgive.

My good friend Caio tells a personal, moving story of that power. I have seen what a beautiful work of restoration God has done in his family. I translated this story from the Portuguese.[1]

MAMA FORGIVES AT CHRISTMASTIME

"She was pretty, there was no denying that. Blond, shapely, provocative, extroverted—she was a Brazilian Marilyn Monroe. She was my father's lover. I saw her for the first time when I was seven years old and vowed that one day I would kill her for what she was doing to my mother.

"As I remember it, Mama seemed to cry most of the time, first sharing her tears with her own mother and then with me. Though I was too young to understand, I could feel all the hurt and humiliation that were now part of her life.

"At home, in the Amazon River city of Manaus, my father and mother went days, weeks, even months without exchanging a word. I became their messenger, asking for money and delivering it, carrying notes, becoming their voice to one another to communicate only the most essential information, nothing more. The more my mother cried, the more cynical my father became.

"Then one day, Mama—although she probably knew she would lose control of her emotions—packed me in the car and took me to visit this woman who had caused us so much pain. I suppose she thought that by taking me, a little boy, along she could convince her rival to leave my father alone. But our visit ended in humiliation when we found the woman in my father's arms. We had no choice but to return home. How I hated that woman for ruining our lives!

"I was already insecure, but things got worse for our family. Dad lost 80 percent of everything he had, and we were forced to move from Manaus to Rio de Janeiro. Dad carried a gun, determined to kill a group of eight men before they could kill him. Every day, I expected to see him carried home in a casket.

"Eventually we moved across the bay to Niteroi, where Dad had a transforming experience with Jesus Christ. At the same time, the grace of Christ met Mom in a new way. Later we moved back to Manaus, where Dad became a minister.

"Although I rebelled for a few years and refused to have anything to do with my parents' faith, Christ eventually brought change into my life, as well. Our family was united in faith and love. At the age of twenty-one, I, too, completed the required studies and was ordained a minister, to serve alongside my father in a large church.

"One day, as I was going to make a pastoral call, I thought of my father's former companion. In my memory she was still beautiful, but how would she be in real life? Was she happy? Had she found another companion? What was she like now?

"I drove by the beauty parlor she owned. Then, looking

toward the shop, I heard an inner voice say, 'Go back and see her.'

"I couldn't believe what I was hearing and feeling. The wound was reopened in my soul, and I struggled, saying, 'God, don't you know I was just going to drive by this place? Couldn't you find someone else to share the gospel with this woman?' But the conviction wouldn't go away: 'Go in and talk to her. Treat her as if she were your own mother.'

"Reluctantly, I stopped the car to pray. Tears came to my eyes as I resisted the impulse of God's Spirit. Finally I said, 'All right, Lord, I'll go.' I got out and, standing at the door of the salon, I could see her across the room.

"She was still pretty, about fifty, I thought, but very attractive.

"She looked up and recognized me at once. 'You're Dr. Caio's son, aren't you?'

" 'Yes, ma'am, I am.'

" 'You're the preacher on the TV show. I've been watching you.'

" 'Yes.'

" 'You must hate me,' she said.

" 'No, much to the contrary. I've come here to tell you that I love you and I want to respect you like I do my own mother.'

"Hearing those words, she began to weep and, as I saw her tears, my eyes filled, too. Clinging to me, she led the way to a small room behind the salon where she confessed, 'I'm a disgrace. I've spent my whole life ruining marriages, destroying families—not just yours—there are others. My life is a hell. I'm all alone. No one wants me. No one respects me.'

"I listened to her and felt pity. When she had finished talking, I excused myself and went straight to my parents' home. I asked Mama and Dad if we could go into their bedroom to talk. There in the quietness of their most intimate setting, we talked about how God had come into our lives and changed the direction of our family. They both rejoiced with me as we all remembered what God had done.

" 'But,' I said, 'what about that woman? We're happy, but she's not. Is she going to have to remain in her miserable spiritual condition forever?'

"My mother interrupted me. 'No! I pray for her every day. I want her to be saved.'

" 'Then you ought to share the gospel with her,' I said too quickly.

"Mama answered immediately. 'Oh, son, I pray that God will use someone else, because it's too hard for me. She robbed me of my very life. She took years away from me. I have no hatred toward her, but I can't love her like I know I should. That's why I ask Jesus to send someone else.'

" 'Well then,' I answered, 'God has already answered your prayers, because I went to see her. I told her I want to love her like I love you. She says she would like to see you but is too ashamed. I invited her to church, but out of respect for you, she says she will not come.'

"Mama was not prepared for that. She answered, 'That's asking too much of me. I can't do it.'

"Disappointed, I said nothing more but began visiting my new friend regularly. I read the Bible and prayed with her almost daily for nearly two months."

THEN IT WAS CHRISTMAS

"Christmas was always special at our house, because it was just one week before that wonderful celebration that Dad had given his heart to the Lord. Now it was Christmas Eve and the whole family was gathered together—brothers, sisters, wives, children, Mama and Dad.

"I knew that the Holy Spirit had been speaking to Mama, and I thought she might be ready to face her former adversary. 'Mom,' I asked, 'could we all join together as a family choir and go over to her house to sing for her?'

"Mama hesitated, but her resistance was gone. 'Yes, son,'

I heard her agree. 'We can go.' With her consent, we practiced three hymns and drove to the woman's house.

"It was dark when we arrived there, so we stopped outside the gate and began to sing.

"As our voices reached up to her window, it opened just a crack. I could see her shadow. She was watching and listening.

"Then the light came on. Soon she was at the door. Her face was bathed in the softly glowing light. Mom took a step toward her, a step of faith and obedience. Then the woman who had hurt Mom so deeply took a step toward her, and suddenly, somewhere between the gate and the door, they embraced with tears running down their faces.

"We kept singing of the Prince of Peace while they hugged and kissed and washed away their pain in the tears of forgiveness.

"Then it was Dad's turn. No one objected when he hugged her. It wasn't the hug of a lover; it was the hug of a friend.

"And they are still friends. *We* are still friends—Mama, Dad, me, my whole family, and the woman I had wanted to kill. We love each other and care for each other as true friends should."

Trust God to make forgiveness work. Even if the person does not respond, you will gain a victory for doing your part.

" 'AS THE FATHER HAS SENT ME, I NOW SEND YOU.... IF YOU FORGIVE ANYONE HIS SINS, THEY ARE FORGIVEN; IF YOU DO NOT FORGIVE THEM, THEY ARE NOT FORGIVEN.' "

JOHN 20:21, 23

WHOM SHOULD
WE FORGIVE?

EVERYONE NEEDS TO BE FORGIVEN and to forgive.
Christ wants to use us to take forgiveness to the world. Where
do we start?

PERHAPS WE SHOULD
START BY FORGIVING GOD

"Wait a minute!" you object. "God has done no wrong and
has made no mistakes. God does not need our forgiveness!"
I agree, but *for our sakes* we may need to forgive Him. Please
read on.

Although in our minds we accept that God is absolutely
righteous, holy, loving, just, faithful, merciful, and blameless

in all his ways—in our hearts we may hold conscious or unconscious grudges toward Him for the way He has made us or for things He has allowed to happen.

We read Romans 8:28—*"And we know that in all things God works for the good of those who love him, who have been called according to his purpose"*—and we wonder what's gone wrong.

What's good about this? Haven't I been called? What's His purpose?

The truth is, His purpose is higher than ours and we don't understand it.

It sometimes requires hard times for us to decide to rise to His purpose.

He actually reveals the purpose of verse 28 in verse 29: "For those God foreknew he also predestined to be conformed to the likeness of his Son, that he might be the firstborn among many brothers."

God works in us to make us more like Christ—patient, holy, and surrendered to His will. The difficulties we face become the tools He uses to achieve the purpose He has for us. The sooner we understand that and surrender our lives to His leading, the sooner our purpose will align with His purpose and He will have freedom to do what will be for our highest good.

To prevent all suffering, God would have to abandon His highest purpose or violate our free will or the free will of others who intentionally or unintentionally hurt people. None of us would like to be a marionette with God pulling every string. We cherish the ability to choose our actions. But to have that freedom, we must also be willing to live with the consequences of our freedom and the freedoms of others.

That freedom results in several kinds of suffering:

—WE MAKE WRONG CHOICES AND SUFFER AS A RESULT OF THEM.

—WE MAKE WRONG CHOICES, AND OTHERS SUFFER AS A RESULT OF THEM.

—OTHER PEOPLE MAKE WRONG CHOICES AND SUFFER BECAUSE OF THEM.

—OTHER PEOPLE MAKE WRONG CHOICES, AND WE SUFFER BECAUSE OF THEM.

—WE SUFFER AND OTHERS SUFFER FOR UNEXPLAINABLE REASONS.

We can also be assured that suffering was a normal part of our Savior's life and had a vital role to play in His development.

....

*"He was despised and rejected by men, a man of sorrows,
and familiar with suffering"* (ISAIAH 53:3).

*"In bringing many sons to glory, it was fitting that God,
for whom and through whom everything exists, should make
the author of their salvation perfect through suffering"*
(HEBREWS 2:10).

....

WHO'S RESPONSIBLE FOR WHAT?

After a solitary dinner in a Santiago, Chile, hotel, I talked with
a waiter who said, "I cannot believe in a God of love."

I asked him what had happened to destroy his faith.

"Last Monday night," he said, "I went at 11:00 p.m. to catch
my bus home from work. At the bus stop, I found a person
stretched out under a bench, trying to sleep. My first reaction
was, 'A God of love wouldn't let that happen; therefore, there
is no God of love.' As the week went by, I saw that person each
night and my anger grew steadily. Friday night it came to a
boil when I discovered the person was a woman. A God of love
would not allow that to happen to a woman."

I thought to myself, "How interesting. Five nights in a
row he sees that woman lying there but does nothing to help.

When he finally does react, it's just to raise his fist and blame God."

Friends, something is wrong with our thinking. So often when we say, "God, why don't you *do* something?" God is saying, "And why don't *you* do something?"

GOD IS GRIEVED

God, I believe, was grieved more deeply about the woman's situation then the waiter was and—all-knowing as He is—is grieved simultaneously by millions of situations that are more painful than anything the waiter had ever seen or imagined.

What grieves God? One thing that must grieve Him is the fact that He has entrusted His work to us, His people, and we fail to identify or carry out our responsibilities. The guilt is not God's; it is ours!

Although we should respond to human need and never become indifferent, God knows why that woman was under the bench. It's possible that in her journey toward the Lord or her flight from Him, that was the best place she could possibly be.

Why do we hold grudges against God? Often it's because we are resisting Him or do not understand what God is really like. Subconsciously we superimpose the face of another authority figure upon God's face: "I might have known; God is just like my Dad (or my teacher or my coach or my boss!)."

Maybe "forgiving God" isn't the best way to say it, but we need to clear Him of whatever charges we hold against Him and offer Him the love He deserves. We need to stop standing in judgment of Him. We need to correct our thinking and seek to know Him better. We need to rid ourselves of grudges that we have held against Him.

FORGIVING PARENTS

My father's story is a sad one. Because his father was hard on him, he ran away from home at the age of fifteen, stole a car, and drove it across the state line into Iowa, where he was arrested. Not wanting to be sent home and having no documents, he lied about his age, stating that he was eighteen. He was placed in an adult prison where he often proved to be incorrigible. That resulted in a prolonged sentence, and he was released seven years later.

After he married, he vowed that none of his sons would spend time behind bars. That, of course, was a correct desire, but his way of preventing our imprisonment was wrong. He turned our home into a prison! All five of us brothers—George, Doug, Burt, Bart, and Ken (in order of age)—had to forgive

Dad and deal with personal traumas related to him. Here's what we have to say about forgiveness:

GEORGE—"When I was sixteen, I was as angry with Dad as he had been with his father. One cold Saturday night I did what he most feared: I caught a ride with a trucker headed for South Dakota. As I rode down the highway toward what I imagined to be freedom from his overbearing ways, I thought about three things: What would I do with my life? What would happen if Dad caught up with me? How could I put Mom through so much suffering?

"I came to my senses and went to my maternal grandparents' home. The next day they took me to church, and, believe it or not, I heard the sermon of the prodigal son (see Luke 15:11–32). Then Grandpa negotiated a peaceful return home for me, and Dad became a bit more permissive. We tried harder to communicate with each other. A year later I went to college in Kentucky, and during that year, things came to a head at home. One day Dad doubled his fist to hit Doug in the face. Doug avoided the blow and landed one of his own, knocking Dad to the floor. When Dad got up, he walked out the door and never came back. Since I was a few hundred miles from home (and was relieved that Dad would not be there when I returned), I no longer felt threatened.

"I forgave Dad but always dreaded the excessively dramatic occasions when we would be together. When Dolly and I were leaving for Brazil as missionaries, Dad shook my hand and said he knew he would never see me again. He was right. Less than four months later, he was killed in an accident. My pain and bitterness were gone by then. I was sorry to hear that he had died and hoped that he had made his peace with God, but I never really missed him or mourned for him."

DOUG—"Did I forgive him? Yes! I did share my testimony with him, but I don't remember his saying anything afterward. I tried to show him forgiveness by going to his apartment; repairing, tuning, and putting brakes on his car; and listening patiently to his loud pipe-organ music. If I had told him that I forgave him, he would have had to admit that he did something wrong, and that wasn't going to happen. I prayed for him a lot.

"I think he respected me more after I stood up to him. I don't want to be a hero for something that I did wrong, and I am not proud of that day. That was before I received Christ into my life.

"About a year before Dad was killed, I talked to Rev. Griffith, our former pastor, and told him that I had never heard Dad say one good thing about me in his life. He said that Dad bragged about all of us to him. I know Dad had problems, and I don't harbor anything against him."

BURT—"Mom told me that when I was just a little boy, Dad would hit me and I would go flying across the room. Later I was struck down by an automobile and had a skull fracture and a serious concussion. After that, Dad changed his tactics. Instead of hitting me, he used verbal abuse: 'You'll never amount to a hill of beans. All your brains leaked out through the hole in your head.' Growing up, I tried to stay clear of him and not be noticed.

"Memories of the abuse haunted me for fifty-five years, and when I talked about it with friends, they suggested that I drive from my home in Minneapolis to his gravesite in North Dakota and say what I had to say. Forty years from the day of his death, I got in my car, rehearsing in my mind the words I would use. When I finally arrived, I shut off the engine, opened the door, and set my feet on the ground. I went to his grave and returned some of the verbal abuse that he had given me. I told him I *did* amount to something. Finally I spat on his grave, closed the car door, and drove away. About halfway between Jamestown and Valley City, North Dakota, God's Spirit spoke to me: 'You forgot something.' I knew immediately what it was, and I finally said the most important words of the seven-hundred-mile trip—'I forgive you!' "

BART—"I hated Dad for the humiliation and outbursts of violence that occurred so often. I used to pray that something would happen to him. An accident was the preferable means in my eight- or-nine-year-old mind.

"Later, after becoming a Christian, I started praying for the members of our family. Eventually I prayed for Dad. I tried to tell him that I had asked Jesus to be my Savior, but he never let me dwell on the subject.

"The last time I saw Dad alive was on Father's Day 1967, when I was eighteen years old. Soon after that, I was teaching Vacation Bible School for the American Sunday School Union. The missionary called me out of class and told me that Dad had been killed in an auto accident the day before. After hearing the news, I walked for a while, finally arrived at the home where I was staying, threw myself on the bed, and wept for a long time. I had never told Dad that I forgave him.

"I was like a walking time bomb. Every now and then, there would be a minor explosion and I would have to apologize to someone. A psychologist asked me about Dad, and I realized that—though I had volitionally forgiven him (out of Christian duty)—I still harbored resentment inside of me. The psychologist helped me get rid of a lot of pent-up violence.

"He also helped me forgive a man who had angered and humiliated me. I told him about the situation, and he suggested a role play: 'I'll be the offender, and you tell me everything that is wrong with me.' I agreed, so he listened patiently while I spewed out a long list of the man's shortcomings. When I finished, he looked me in the eyes and asked, 'Is there anything else?' I said, 'No.' Then he surprised me by saying, 'You're absolutely right about all my defects. Will you please forgive me?'

"I had prepared myself to argue for my point of view, but I was not prepared for this. After a long pause, I told him I would forgive him. But he was not through with me yet. He asked, 'Will you pray for me right now?' Reluctantly I placed my hands on his shoulders and prayed for his forgiveness. He did the same for me.

"All of a sudden, I was aware of my own shortcomings and what a difficult person I had been. I felt so badly that I wrote a letter of apology to the offender. He never answered me, but nine years later when I saw him again, he was very warm toward me.

"I also learned to forgive. One evening when our daughter Sharon was nine, she was not quite sassy but very indifferent toward me. I took her into the next room and asked her if she thought maybe she had been a little hard on her daddy. I waited for her to make things right, but she said, 'No, I don't think so.' I waited a little longer and finally said, 'I guess you might as well go to bed then.'

"Walking her to the stairs, I watched her go up to her room. I waited at the foot of the stairs for about ten minutes, thinking she would come down, throw her arms around my neck, and say she was sorry. It was a long ten minutes, and I finally realized she wasn't coming. Before I walked away, though, I felt that God was saying to me, 'I know...' And I could visualize God waiting at the stairs for me and for 5 billion other people to come back and say 'I'm sorry.' He didn't wait with a raised fist, as some people imagine, but with open arms. He would take them all unconditionally, the way I would with Sharon."

KEN—"I can't say that Dad didn't have an impact on me. I'm sure he was a large part of shaping me at that young age. My mode to deal with him was silence. In fact, I didn't speak to anyone I didn't trust, so my brothers and my mother knew my voice, but very few others ever heard me speak a word until I was in the third grade. I even made up words that only my family understood.

"Hospitalized with rheumatic fever at age five and then placed in a psychiatric hospital to discover the source of my emotional problems, I wasn't released until my father had left the home for good.

"I believe that forgiveness comes naturally to children. It takes years to learn that our power to forgive can be held back to inflict pain on the object of our unforgiveness. Having been convinced by many voices that I should hate and reject my father, I eventually gave in. He was the invisible object of my anger and scorn. It wasn't until long after he was gone that, on one particular occasion when I was subjected to loud organ music, a response was triggered in me that I didn't even know was there. For the first time I wept for my father, and I made a decision to forgive him and put that pain behind me. My hope is that he did have a saving knowledge of Christ."

It is not easy to forgive dysfunctional parents. They leave scars upon us, and we discover that the deeper the scars, the harder it is to forgive. But whatever it takes, it is worth the effort to bring healing between parents and children. The last promise of the Old Testament shows God's concern for reestablishing this relationship:

> *"I will send you Elijah the prophet.... Elijah will help parents love their children and children love their parents"* (MALACHI 4:56).

BROTHERS AND SISTERS

The earliest families on record experienced serious conflicts between siblings. Cain was so jealous of Abel's faith and acceptance before God that he murdered him. Jacob took advantage of his twin brother Esau's hunger to rob him of his birthright. Later he deceived his father, Isaac, and cheated Esau out of the family blessing, as well. Then Jacob ran for his life. Jacob married first Leah and then Rachel, sisters who were bitterly jealous of each other. Jacob's sons sold his favorite son Joseph as a slave to Egypt. These were not happy families.

Hurtful words are spoken, and humiliating things happen between brothers and sisters that can result in lifelong grudges. Some resent having to live up to their older sibling's reputation—whether good or bad. Others feel that favoritism has been shown. Much long-standing resentment could be cleared up if brothers and sisters would open up with each other, talk things out, and forgive the hurts of the past.

My good friend Dick had terribly hurtful experiences as a child. His mother died in childbirth, and he was shuffled back and forth between home and an orphanage until he didn't know where he belonged. Eventually, he was taken in by a brother and his young wife.

Dick's sister-in-law tried her best to help him, but she didn't know how to handle a small boy. Dick was often told that if he misbehaved, he would be thrown out of the home. "And then where will you go? Nobody wants you, you know." Birthdays were horrible for Dick. Each year someone reminded him that if it weren't for his birth, his mother would still be alive.

It was a wonderful day when Dick invited Christ into his life. He learned to feel at home in the family of God. Called to be a missionary, Dick attended a Bible college, where he learned to walk with God and correct the wrongs he had done in the past. Remembering the spiteful things he did to get even with his sister-in-law, Dick wrote a letter asking for her forgiveness. When she read the letter, she was so moved that she framed it and became extremely proud of Dick. Eventually Dick became a missionary and served as a valuable member of a Bible institute staff.

Dick has shared his story many times, and it has always been a great encouragement to people. But he and his wife, Bernice, noticed that each time he told the story, he would weep painfully.

In 1977, Dick and Bernice attended a seminar and received prayer for healing of the memories. Though Dick was not asked to specify or relive his traumas, the seminar leaders seemed to receive special insight from God. While praying with Dick, they were enabled by the Holy Spirit to cite specific moments in Dick's life when he had been hurt. They asked God to walk through the corridors of Dick's mind and heal every hurtful place.

He has never again been troubled by painful memories. He can now look back on those experiences with no heartache or bitterness. He has not forgotten the events but neither is he disturbed by any of them. Dick and Bernice have a happy marriage and two grown children who serve the Lord. To see Dick and his family together, you would never suspect that he had suffered so much as a child. He is healed.

SPOUSES AND FORMER SPOUSES

J. Allen Peterson, a well-known Christian marriage counselor, described in a talk a treatment used by a colleague when all other techniques failed:

A woman went to a counselor's office and said, "It's all over. I can't take it anymore. I want a divorce immediately."

In a last effort, the counselor asked, "Are you going to let him off that easy? You should make him suffer first before you send him away."

"How can I do that?" the lady asked.

"First, you have to convince him that you really love him. It will take you about a month, but here's what I want you to do. Go home and get into your best dress. Meet him at the door and tell him that you love him. Have his favorite dinner waiting for him. Try every day to do something special, and make him feel like a king. At the end of thirty days, tell him it was all a big act, that you can't stand him, and that you want a divorce."

Her desire for vengeance was so great that she decided to do it. Right away she began acting out the role of a loving wife. She literally spoiled her husband, doing everything she could to please him.

After thirty days, the counselor called to ask how things were going: "Do you still want to go through with the divorce?"

"Divorce?" she exclaimed. "I never wanted a divorce. My husband has been so kind for the past month that I could never think about leaving him. He's the sweetest man in the world!"

What happened? At first she had no feelings of love and forgiveness, but she acted as though she did. He warmed to her affection and began to fulfill her expectations. Gradually her feelings of affection returned, and she was able to fulfill his expectations, as well. They fell deeply in love.

Many times love and forgiveness need to be acted out as a choice of the will rather than fluttering emotions.

FORGIVING A DIVORCE

I can't believe that God requires a person to continue in a marriage if it means danger to one's physical well-being or if continual unfaithfulness destroys any possibility of reconciliation. Neither do I believe that an act of unfaithfulness is a call for automatic divorce. It is a call for confrontation, counseling, maybe temporary separation, but above all, a call for repentance, forgiveness, and reconciliation.

In today's culture, divorce has become common among Christians. Thank God, some churches have become effective in reaching those who have gone through the tragedy of divorce. Divorcées must find understanding and forgiveness in the church. But the church must never compromise on God's standards or fail to communicate His disapproval of this social tragedy and sin. Malachi spoke to the problem in strong words in Malachi 2:13–16 NCV:

....

"This is another thing you do. You cover the LORD's altar with tears. You cry and moan, because he does not accept your offerings and is not pleased with what you bring. You ask, 'Why?' It is because the LORD sees how you treated the wife you married when you were young. You broke your promise to her, even though she was your partner and you

had an agreement with her. God made husbands and wives to become one body and one spirit for his purpose—so they would have children who are true to God. So be careful, and do not break your promise with the wife you married when you were young. The LORD God of Israel says, 'I hate divorce. And I hate people who do cruel things as easily as they put on clothes', says the LORD All-Powerful. So be careful. And do not break your trust."

Since God takes our marriage vows seriously, we cannot pass over them lightly. "Until death do us part" is a pledge that eliminates the possibility of divorce except for the exceptions listed above. Neither divorce nor remarriage frees a person from the responsibility to forgive and seek forgiveness.

FORGIVENESS BETWEEN NATIONS

Paraguay is a small South American nation with a population of 3 million bilingual people speaking Guarani and Spanish. (Spanish is the trade language; Guarani is the heart language.)

Paraguay once fought a war against Brazil, Argentina, and Uruguay all at the same time. Paraguay had become an advanced civilization. South America's first railroad was built in Paraguay.

The agriculture economy thrived. Laws were enforced, and crime was practically unknown.

But the thriving country was a threat to other nations, and the War of the Triple Alliance resulted, killing more than 90 percent of Paraguay's adult males and enormous numbers of women and children. History tells of six-year-old boys bearing arms to defend their country and dying in battle. Pregnant women were shot in the womb. Large portions of Paraguay's land were seized by Brazil.

An important statue now stands between the Paraguayan national airport and the capital city of Asunción. It depicts a mother and her child standing beside a fallen husband. Paraguayans have never forgotten that war.

THE CHURCH CAN HAVE A PART IN SOLVING NATIONAL PROBLEMS

During a teaching session in the Paraguayan city of Encarnación, I talked about these historical facts with the young people—Brazilian, Paraguayans, and Argentines. I suggested that it would be wonderful to bring representatives of these people together for a moment of reconciliation.

Myriam, a young Argentine girl who grew up in Paraguay,

shared the idea with Christian leaders. They, in turn, called Paraguayan, Argentinean, Brazilian, and Uruguayan missionaries to a prayer encounter on one of the main plazas of Asunción. About 3,000 people watched the missionaries, each carrying the flag of his own offending nation, ask forgiveness of the Paraguayan people. Prayer was then offered for healing of relationships while Paraguayan believers stood in the plaza and wept. Forgiveness flowed between Christians of the four nations, and people reconsecrated their lives to the Lord.

A few months after this forgiveness encounter took place, I sat alongside a Paraguayan government official on a flight between major cities in Brazil. I told him that I loved Paraguay and knew what a terrible injustice had been committed against his nation. Then I told him how the Christians had gathered to ask for forgiveness. To my surprise, the official, with tears in his eyes, invited me to his home the next time I should visit his nation.

Because Christ has made it possible for all barriers to be broken down, let us take the message of forgiveness and reconciliation to all the nations of the world for the sake of Christ and his kingdom and forgive everyone.

THERE IS A TIME
TO FORGIVE AND A
TIME TO CONFRONT.
THERE IS ALSO A
TIME TO CONFRONT
AND FORGIVE.

CARING ENOUGH TO
RISK CONFRONTATION

YES, THE PROBLEM had gone on too long, but it was not an easy one to deal with. How do you face the head of a nation with the double accusation of adultery and murder—if you value your own life? Many prayers for wisdom, grace, and protection must have gone up to God before the prophet Nathan appeared in David's throne room in 2 Samuel 12 (NCV) to confront the king:

....

" *There were two men in a city. One was rich, but the other was poor. The rich man had many sheep and cattle. But the poor man had nothing except one little female lamb he had bought. The poor man fed the lamb, and it grew up with*

him and his children. It shared his food and drank from his
cup and slept in his arms. The lamb was like a daughter to him.
Then a traveler stopped to visit the rich man. The rich man
wanted to feed the traveler, but he didn't want to take one of
his own sheep or cattle. Instead, he took the lamb from the poor
man and cooked it for his visitor.' "

....

Yes, David was angry, but his anger was not directed at Nathan;
he was angry with the rich man in the story. Completely absorbed
and thoroughly disgusted, David pronounced to Nathan:

....

" *'As surely as the* LORD *lives, the man who did this should*
die! He must pay for the lamb four times for doing such a thing.
He had no mercy!' "

....

David, the highest authority in Israel, determined a stiff
sentence for a cowardly crime. What he didn't know was that
he was declaring himself guilty of a much greater offense. For
it was at this moment that Nathan, the faithful and courageous
prophet, declared:

....

" *'You are the man!'...* ' "*You killed Uriah...and took his wife*
to become your wife.... You did not respect [God]; you took

the wife of Uriah the Hittite.... You had sexual relations with Bathsheba in secret but [God] will [punish you publicly] so all the people of Israel can see it." ' "

What daring accusations! What courage! There was no mistaking what the case was all about, but what would David's reaction be?

" 'I have sinned against the Lord.' "

In the secrecy of his private world, David must have confessed his sin a thousand times during the nine months of Bathsheba's pregnancy. As the baby grew in her womb, his conviction of sin must have grown, too. He must have shuddered before the God he had always served when Joab sent word that the murder of Uriah was accomplished. He must have groaned inwardly in shame when Bathsheba moved in with him. He would acknowledge his sin painfully when the baby died, but until that moment he had kept it to himself.

Referring to this period of time, which possibly lasted up to a year, David confessed:

"When I kept things to myself, I felt weak deep inside me. I moaned all day long. Day and night you punished me.

My strength was gone as in the summer heat. Selah"

(PSALM 32:3–4 NCV).

. . . .

But now he was being confronted with his guilt and resulting chastisement by a respected man of God. Amazingly, along with the accusation came the positive word, "The LORD has taken away your sin" (2 Samuel 12:13 NCV). Amazing also was the effect the confrontation had in David's life—acknowledgment of sin, brokenness, repentance, chastisement, and then restoration. Without a doubt, that was a wise and effective confrontation.

DO I REALLY HAVE TO CONFRONT?

Very few people in this world enjoy confronting others about their sins, misunderstandings, or disagreements. (Those who really enjoy it should probably ask themselves why they do.) Most of us will go to any length necessary to avoid confrontation.

Yet scripture makes it clear that we Christians should gently, lovingly, yet boldly—confront other believers who sin against us or who are involved in wrongdoing. " 'If your brother sins, rebuke him, and if he repents, forgive him' " (Luke 17:3).

Peter must have learned something about confrontation; he was confronted by both Jesus and Paul:

....

"Jesus said to Peter, 'Go away from me, Satan! You are not helping me! You don't care about the things of God, but only about the things people think are important' " (MATTHEW 16:23 NCV).

"A third time [Jesus] said, 'Simon son of John, do you love me?' Peter was hurt because Jesus asked him the third time.... Peter said, 'Lord, you know everything; you know that I love you!' " (JOHN 21:17 NCV).

"I spoke to Peter in front of them all. I said, 'Peter, you are a Jew, but you are not living like a Jew. You are living like those who are not Jewish. So why do you now try to force those who are not Jewish to live like Jews?' " (GALATIANS 2:14 NCV).

....

The confrontations had their desired effect. Peter became a great man of God and a wonderful encourager of the church.

FOLLOWING SCRIPTURE IN CONFRONTATION

A Brazilian Christian came into my office weeping. He said he had been mercilessly humiliated by a missionary in front of his colleagues.

My first reaction was like David's—empathy and anger. I had taken up other people's causes in the past and gotten in trouble for it. Foolishly, I was ready to do it again. But this time, before I could do anything to compound the problem, I remembered Matthew 18:15–20:

....

" 'If your fellow believer sins against you, go and tell him in private what he did wrong. Do this in private. If he listens to you, you have helped that person to be your brother or sister again. But if he refuses to listen, go to him again and take one or two other people with you. "Every case may be proved by two or three witnesses." If he refuses to listen to them, tell the church. If he refuses to listen to the church, then treat him like a person who does not believe in God or like a tax collector.' "

....

I read that passage of scripture to my friend and said, "I'm going to ask you to do the hardest thing you could possibly do. Go tell that man that he hurt you. Tell him how humiliated you felt. Tell him how unfair he was to you. And tell him that you are coming to forgive him; extend an invitation to acknowledge his sin and repent. If he doesn't respond as he should, you come back to me and we'll go together."

After he left my office, I prepared myself for the encounter that seemed inevitable. But when my friend returned a couple of hours later, he beamed and said, "I've won a brother."

It's always nice to tell a success story, but so often we fail. Instead of talking to the offender, we talk to others behind his or her back. Besides involving others in troubles that are not theirs, we slander the reputation of our offenders. Then our anger grows, and we put ourselves into a position before others where we feel we can't back down. Or we use a wrong process to work out the problem.

HOW OFTEN WE FAIL TO CONFRONT WHEN WE SHOULD!

I was once involved in a confrontation where we needed to bring two Christian brothers together with a group of elders who sought to bring them to reconciliation. One of the elders had clearly and compassionately stated the errors that one of the men had committed and helped him to see what he needed to do to correct his error.

In the course of the discussion, it became apparent that I, as leader of the group, should have taken action sooner, before the problem grew into a major conflict.

The same elder then turned to me and said lovingly, "George, you're my friend, and I love you. But you let these situations go on too long. When you see that a problem exists, you need to step in and deal with it." In Ephesians 4:15, Paul wrote, "We will speak the truth in love, growing in every way more and more like Christ." My friend was right about my failure to deal quickly with many issues, and he was right about facing me with it. It is Christlike to lovingly confront each other with the truth. It is a sign of maturity. I recognized my fault and appreciated having it clarified.

OBEDIENCE WORKS!

A missionary once complained to me, "One of my board members is trying to walk off with the business. I've talked to him. Others have talked to him. It looks like I'll have to take him to court."

I hated to see that happen. Scripture admonishes us not to take a brother to a civil court (1 Corinthians 6:1–11). So I said, "Why don't you take the matter to his church? Explain to the pastor that you have done everything you know to do and everything the Bible requires, but nothing has worked. Ask for his help."

Several weeks later, the missionary told me, "That was the best advice I ever received. The pastor got a group of leaders together and examined the situation, and the whole problem has been worked out."

HOW TO CONFRONT

When Paul exhorted the Galatian Christians to confront erring brothers, he gave them some guidelines:

....

"Brothers and sisters, if someone in your group does something wrong, you who are spiritual should go to that person and gently help him make him right again. But be careful, because you might be tempted to sin, too. By helping each other with your troubles, you truly obey the law of Christ.... Each person should judge his own actions" (GALATIANS 6:1–2, 4 NCV).

....

"YOU WHO ARE SPIRITUAL..." Confrontation is clearly a job for those who are spiritually sensitive and whose lives are in order. Jesus said, " 'How can you say to your brother, "Let me take the speck out of your eye," when all the time there is a plank in your own eye?' " (Matthew 7:4).

"HELP MAKE HIM RIGHT AGAIN." The objective is restoration, not just correction. If you don't have the right motive in mind, you are not ready to get involved.

"GENTLY..." So many situations are volatile. A harshly spoken or untrue word can cause an explosion that could put things out of place forever. "A gentle answer will calm a person's anger, but an unkind answer will cause more anger" (Proverbs 15:1).

"HELP EACH OTHER." The Christian life wasn't designed to be lived alone. We need to be supportive, not judgmental, when our friends are struggling with sin in their lives.

"EACH PERSON SHOULD JUDGE HIS OWN ACTIONS." Beware of assuming a position of superiority. Remember that no one is exempt from temptation. It could be you next time.

A CASE FOR CONFRONTATION

Richard Duncan, a former missionary in Brazil with O.C. International and now a pastor in California, has developed a series of studies concerning the ministry of confrontation.[1] He reminds us that confrontation is necessary when a person is headed for destruction.

....

" 'Suppose I [God] say to the wicked: "Wicked people, you will surely die," but you don't speak to warn the wicked to stop doing evil. Then they will die because they were sinners but I will punish you for their deaths" (EZEKIEL 33:8).

....

Then Duncan shares a series of tests to use when deciding whether the situation calls for confrontation. The text below is translated from the Portuguese and was slightly adapted:

1. THE TEST OF LOVE. Do I really care about this individual and want to help him? Do I love him enough to be patient, kind, and forgiving?

2. THE TEST OF TRUTH. Do I know the truth about the situation? Is there specific Bible teaching about this issue?

3. THE TEST OF NECESSITY. Is the situation serious enough to demand a confrontation? What will happen if the situation continues as it is?

4. THE TEST OF WORDS. Have I thought this situation thoroughly so that I really know what I'm talking about? Does it call for some creativity like Nathan used?

5. THE TEST OF TIME. Is this the right time to deal with the situation? Is the person ready to face it? What kind of mood will I find the person in? How can I arrange the best possible circumstances that will contribute toward a successful encounter?

A WOUND THAT HEALS

Those few people in this world who love to confront often seem to enjoy a fight and take pleasure in showing their power. They can be cruel and sarcastic. How do you like this kind of approach?—"Why don't you grow up? Why don't you get with it? If you don't produce, you'll be fired. You're not irreplaceable, you know. Some people around here just don't carry their part of the load. Shape up or ship out. Can't you do anything right? You lied; you're wrong; that's sin! How do you expect God to bless you when you act like that?"

Some only confront when they are angry, but an angry confrontation often does more harm than good. Yet the errors that others commit in poor confrontations should not prevent us from doing what must be done. Confrontation can be done in a friendly way: "My brother, could I talk with you alone for a few minutes? It's out of love and appreciation that I would like to share something I have noticed that you may not be aware of, and that could damage your relationship with the Lord and your ministry to others. Can we talk about it?"

David Augsburger points out that many see caring and confrontations mutually exclusive. "There is a time for caring and a time for confrontation. To confront powerfully, lay care aside. To care genuinely, candor and confrontation must be forgotten for the moment at least."

Augsburger then suggests a third word: "Care-frontation unifies concern for relationship with concerns for goals, so one can have something to stand for (goals) as well as someone to stand with (relationships) without sacrificing one for the other or collapsing one with the other."[2]

Confrontation is not sign of animosity; it's a sign of true friendship, as the scripture says:

....

"It is better to correct someone openly than to have love and not show it. The slap of a friend can be trusted to help you, but the kisses of an enemy are nothing but lies" (PROVERBS 27:5–6).

....

THIS IS GOING TO HURT ME MORE THAN IT DOES YOU, BUT...

Confronting is seldom a pleasant task. It requires love, wisdom, discernment, courage, and gentleness. It also requires that we be open to having our lives examined and corrected by others. We run the risk of being involved in a process that is as painful to us as it is to the person confronted.

The goals are to benefit the person and to bring about reconciliation when possible. Are those worthwhile goals? Then maybe the risk is worth taking.

" 'A THIEF COMES
TO STEAL AND KILL
AND DESTROY,
BUT I CAME TO GIVE LIFE—
LIFE IN ALL ITS FULLNESS.' "

JOHN 10:10 NCV

IT'S TIME TO
LIVE ABUNDANTLY

THE ABUNDANT LIFE that Jesus came to bring is to be lived *in the present tense*! It's not a life that "could have been" or "might someday be"; it's a life for here and now. It's not for an elite class of people; it's for you and me!

OPPOSITION GUARANTEED!

Something so precious as abundant life doesn't come without a price. In the passage above, Jesus not only revealed what He came to provide *for* us; He also warned about what "the thief," Satan, comes to take *from* us. What a stark contrast we find between the two!

SATAN	JESUS
Robs us.	Enriches us.
Cheats us.	Blesses us.
Brings us grief.	Brings us joy.
Deceives us.	Enlightens us.
Drives us.	Leads us.
Enslaves us.	Frees us.
Defeats us.	Empowers us.
Seeks to kill us.	Gives us life.

This promise of abundant life comes at the heart of a message in which Jesus calls himself the "Good Shepherd," who cares every day for his sheep: "He calls his own sheep by name and leads them out. When he brings all his sheep out, he goes ahead of them, and they follow him because they know his voice" (John 10:3–4 NCV).

The Good Shepherd knows us by name and loves us. He laid down his life for us. He calls us to abundant living. He promises to give us hope and a future and to satisfy our spiritual hunger.

SO WHAT KEEPS US FROM THAT LIFE?

I can think of dozens of answers to that question. Satan's opposition is just one of them. Most answers have to do with our lack of hearing, knowing, and following the voice of Jesus. But I want to focus on one specific cause for failure that I see again and again: Often we fail to live the abundant life today because we are *reliving* negative experiences from yesterday and *dreading* or *avoiding repetition* of those experiences tomorrow.

Feelings of sorrow, guilt, shame, rejection, fear, anger, resentment, humiliation, and inadequacy chain us to the past and obstruct our future. Even once actual memories fade or are repressed, we discover within ourselves negative responses and reactions that we still cannot explain to ourselves.

Satan uses our past to effectively block the way to peace, freedom, victory, and the enjoyment of life here and now.

NO GOING BACK. TIME MARCHES ON!

If we could go back in time, we might attempt to avoid the errors we have committed and the painful things that have happened to us. But time tunnels work only in fiction. We may regret bad yesterdays and dream of better tomorrows, but our future is determined by what we do right now. I challenge the idea that "time cures all ills." We need a powerful intervention into our lives that comes not from time but from eternity.

Here's the amazing news: The God who dwells in eternity allowed Himself to be compressed into time in the person of Jesus Christ, His Son, who experienced time as we do and offers us new life—abundant life!—always in the present tense.

....

"If anyone is in Christ, he is a new creation; the old has gone, the new has come!" (2 CORINTHIANS 5:17).

....

Without Jesus, there is nothing new under the sun. With Him we have everything new—new standing, new birth, new life, new peace, new access, new joy, new resilience, new security, new friendship—new life! In Him we are new creations. We know this is true, but sometimes such enthusiastic statements make us nervous. They sound unreal or naive. We become cynical regarding these exciting possibilities.

The word *repentance* is about change—changing our mind, changing behavior, changing allegiance, and changing direction. It's turning 180 degrees away from sin and turning to Jesus.

The word *forgiveness* is about deciding that we are no longer going to hurt, maintain ill feelings, pay back, seek revenge, or even speak negatively about persons who have hurt us—and we are going to accept total forgiveness to such a degree that we forgive also ourselves.

TODAY IS THE DAY!

Wouldn't it be wonderful to live without bitterness, anger, guilt, regrets, fear, addictions, and recurring bondages? Wouldn't we love to find healing for the complex, hurting persons we have become?

God can change us now and in an ongoing process. He can

erase the marks our past has stamped upon us and break the chains that keep us repeating the "same old, same old" again and again. He can remake us into the victorious persons He designed us to be. I love to think about this wonderful truth: God loves me just as I am, but He loves me too much to leave me as I am.

LET GOD RESHAPE YOUR LIFE!

Jeremiah the prophet went to the potter's house to watch him work and then gave this report:

> *"I went down to the potter's house, and I saw him working at the wheel. But the pot he was shaping from the clay was marred in his hands; so the potter formed it into another pot, shaping it as seemed best to him"* (JEREMIAH 18:3–4).

Even though the vessel broke, it never left the potter's hand. He remade it into something beautiful—just as God wants to do with you and me. Even when we feel that our lives have fallen apart, God has a plan for us. He never gives up.

> *"God began doing a good work in you, and I am sure he will continue it until it is finished"* (PHILIPPIANS 1:6 NCV).

EMBRACE THE PRESENT; AIM FOR THE FUTURE

As we know, the apostle Paul was a persecutor of Christians before his conversion to Christ. After Paul met Jesus and began to serve him, his memories could have crippled him with guilt. Yet Paul found freedom through a wonderful formula:

"There is one thing I always do. Forgetting the past and straining toward what is ahead, I keep trying to reach the goal and get the prize for which God called me through Christ to the life above" (PHILIPPIANS 3:13–14 NCV).

These words, though easy to understand, are hard to follow. We forget things we should remember and remember things we should forget. We focus on regrets about the past or fears about the future. We bury memories in convenient places where we can come back to them and use them. We push them back to alleviate pain and pull them out when we feel that we must suffer again or make someone else suffer.

In contrast, King David asked to have his thoughts and sins exposed so he could deal with them in a permanent way:

"Search me, O God, and know my heart; test me and know my anxious thoughts. See if there is any offensive way in me, and lead me in the way everlasting" (PSALM 139:23–24).

When the Holy Spirit shows us our sin, we can confess and repent. When He reveals pain, we can forgive those who have caused it. When we bring closure to our past by confession and repentance, or by forgiveness and reconciliation, then we are ready to move on and receive God's promises.

"The LORD says, Forget what happened before, and do not think about the past. Look at the new thing I am going to do. It is already happening. Don't you see it?" (ISAIAH 43:18–19 NCV).

We can put our past behind us and live in the present enabled by God. We can and *will* see something new that will impact us positively and help us say *yes* to our future!

GRACE TO GET ON WITH LIFE

Today can be the deciding day. You can resign yourself to defeat and unhappiness, or you can choose the abundant life. I offer you six truths to help you start living the abundant life that God intends for you here and now:

1. KNOW THAT JESUS WANTS TO FORGIVE AND HEAL AND RESTORE YOU! No matter what you have done, He can forgive you! No matter what you have suffered, He can heal you! Christ is committed to finishing His work in you! "God began doing a good work in you, and I am sure he will continue it until it is finished" (Philippians 1:6 NCV).

2. CHOOSE RECOVERY. Sure, there are people you could blame, but what good does it do? If they caused you pain, you can't expect them to bring you healing. People may attack you, but they cannot destroy you. "If God is for us, no one can defeat us" (Romans 8:31 NCV). God will put your life back together if you do your part.

3. COMMIT YOUR WHOLE LIFE TO CHRIST. If you have never received Jesus as your Lord and Savior, do it now. Entrust your life to His care and service. "Yet to all who received him, to those who believed in his name, he gave the right to become children of God" (John 1:12).

4. ASK FOR AND EXTEND FORGIVENESS. As you recall your sins, admit your wrongdoing and ask forgiveness. As you recall your pain, forgive those who caused it. "Confess your sins to each other and pray for each other so that you may be healed" (James 5:16 NLT). Be kind and loving to each other, and forgive each other just as God forgave you in Christ" (Ephesians 4:32 NCV).

5. FOLLOW THROUGH. Even after facing your issues, you may be tempted to relive the hurts or blame individuals. Replace those thoughts with correct thinking such as: I have forgiven this person. I no longer blame him or her for my situation. I have been forgiven, too, so I no longer blame myself. I will trust God and get on with my life. When you allow forgiveness to flow from your heart, you replace hostility with love and anxiety with faith, and you are freed from your past. "God's peace...will keep your hearts and minds in Christ Jesus" (Philippians 4:7 NCV).

6. RECLAIM GROUND FROM SATAN. Scripture warns of the harmful effects of sustained anger: "When you are angry, do not sin, and be sure to stop being angry before the end of the day. Do not give the devil a way to defeat you" (Ephesians 4:26–27 NCV). "Give yourselves completely to God. Stand against the devil, and the devil will run from you" (James 4:7 NCV).

This time-tested and proven process demands faith and courage, but Jesus our Savior will help you stand on the forgiveness and acceptance you have in Him. And He will help you grant the same forgiveness to others, leaving your hurts in the past and making abundant living a present reality. God bless you!

NOTES

CHAPTER 3

1. David Seamands, "The Hidden Tormenters," message given at Wilmore United Methodist Church, Wilmore, Kentucky, date unknown.

CHAPTER 5

1. LeRoy Dugan, "Message of the Cross," (Minneapolis: Bethany International, Oct–Dec 1994), 14.

CHAPTER 6

1. Bruce Wilkinson, Secrets of the Vine, Sisters, OR: Multnomah Press, 71.

CHAPTER 7

1. George R. Foster, *O Poder Restaurador do Perdão* [The Healing Power of Forgiveness], (Belo Horizonte, Minas Gerais, Brazil: Editora Betânia, 1993), 136
2. R. T. Kendall, *Total Forgiveness*, (Lake Mary, FL: Charisma House, 2002), 20
3. Kendall, 183–184.

CHAPTER 9

1. Corrie ten Boom with Jamie Buckingham, *Tramp for the Lord, Special Crusade Edition* (Fort Washington, PA: Christian Literature Crusade and Old Tappan, NJ: Fleming H. Revell, 1974), 56.

2. "A Journal of Miracles and Meditations, Hopes and Joys," http://www.miraclesandjoys.com/other-hearts-other-voices/2005/8/13/forgiveness.html. See also ten Boom and Buckingham's *Tramp for the Lord*, 179–180.

CHAPTER 10

1. ten Boom and Buckingham, *Tramp for the Lord*, 181–182.

CHAPTER 11

1. Robert Lowry, "Nothing but the Blood" (1875). www.cyberhymnal.org/htm/r/e/rejtlord.htm

2. R. T. Kendall, *How to Forgive Ourselves—Totally*, (Lake Mary, FL: Charisma House, 2007), 17–30.

3. Seamands, "The Hidden Tormenters," message.

CHAPTER 12

1. Caio Fábio d'Araújo Filho, *Perdão, Encarnação da Graça* [Forgiveness, Incarnation of Grace], (Niteroi, RJ, Brazil, Editora Vinde, 1990).

CHAPTER 14

1. Richard Duncan, *Passo a Passo* [Step by Step], (São Paulo: Sepal, 1990), 89–90.

2. David Augsburger, *The Love Fight*, (Scottsdale, PA: Herald Press, 1983), 9.